A Field Guide to

NEARBY NATURE

Fields and Woods of the Midwest and East Coast

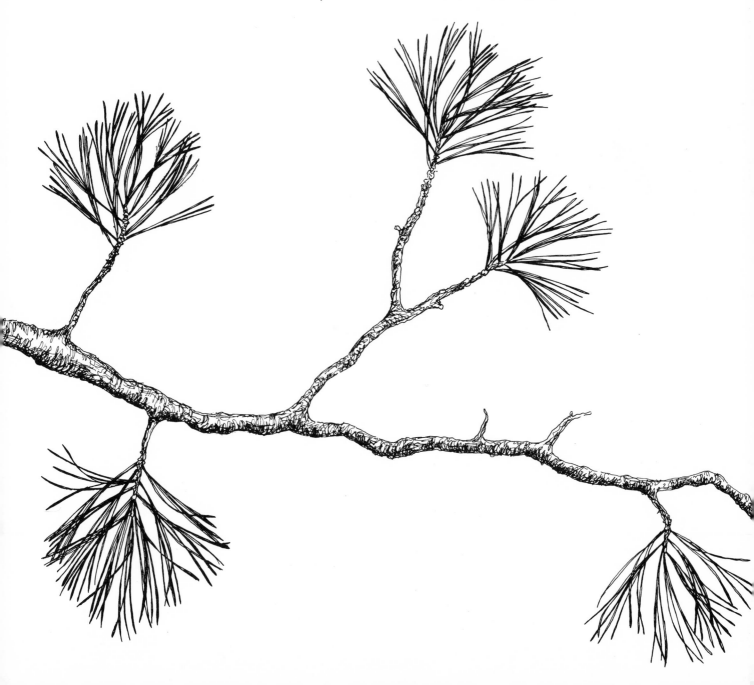

A Field Guide to

NEARBY NATURE

Fields and Woods of the Midwest and East Coast

PEGGY KOCHANOFF

Mountain Press Publishing Company
Missoula, Montana
1994

Library of Congress Cataloging-in-Publication Data

Kochanoff, Peggy, 1943-
    A field guide to nearby nature : fields and woods of the Midwest and East
Coast / Peggy Kochanoff.
        p.   cm.
    Includes bibliographical references (p.   ) and index.
    ISBN 0-87842-299-4 : $14.00
    1. Natural history—Middle West—Juvenile literature.   2. Natural history—East
(U.S.)—Juvenile literature.   3. Natural history—Canada, Eastern—Juvenile
literature.   [1. Natural history.]
    I. Title.
QH104.5.M47K63   1994   94-20762
574.977—dc20   CIP
                                                           AC

PRINTED IN THE U.S.A.

MOUNTAIN PRESS PUBLISHING COMPANY
1301 South Third Street West
Missoula, Montana 59801
(406) 728-1900

Dedicated to my family:
Stan,
Jim,
and Tom

CONTENTS

Many thanks to:

Thelma Bower, a biologist, for checking the accuracy.
Lisa Hines for helping with the graphic setup of the pages.
Peggy Coffill for typing.
My son Jim for typing and computer work.
Peggy Hamilton, my helpful, local librarian.
And my friends and family for their support.

RANGES

The majority of the plants and animals in this book live within the area indicated on this map. The ranges vary, however, especially along the boundary edges.

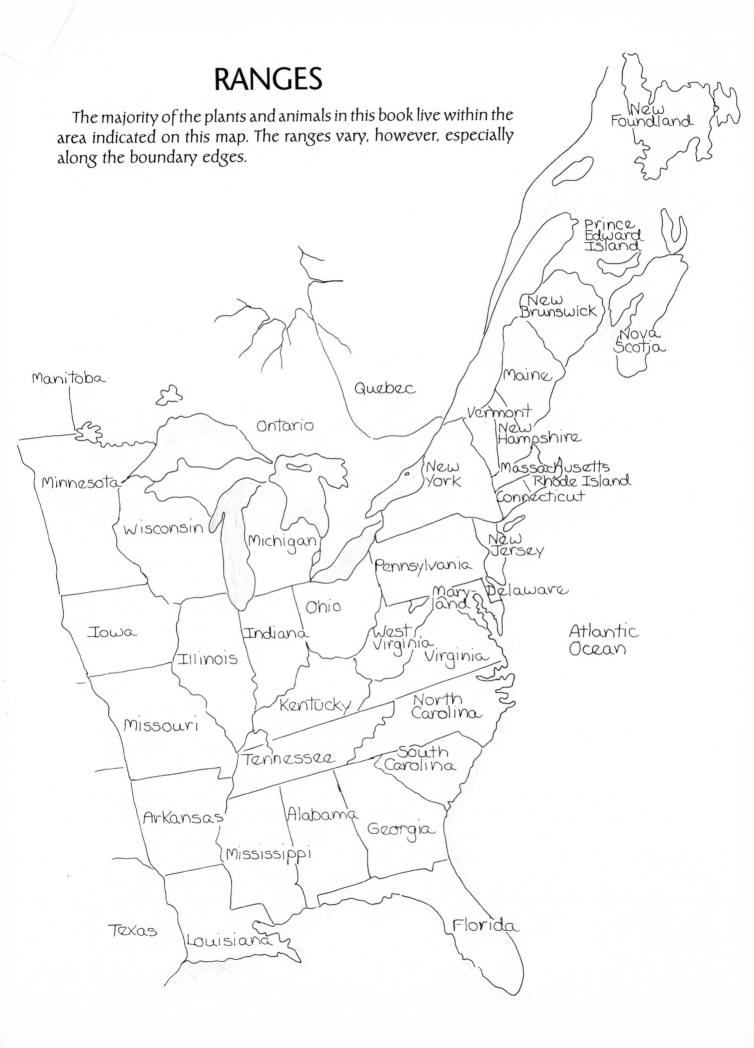

INTRODUCTION

This book is for readers young and old. It explores the living things all around us—under a rock, in a puddle, in the backyard. I hope that spending a few moments watching, touching, listening, or smelling these common plants and animals will help you discover the remarkable and exciting life around you.

The plants and animals in this book can be found from southern Canada through the eastern-central United States—primarily a mixed deciduous forest with a transitional area of evergreens on the edges. Mixed deciduous forest contains mainly broad-leaved trees, such as maples, birch, oak, and beech, that drop their leaves in the fall to survive the cold winter. The region receives measurable moisture as rain or snow over most of the year, so there is rarely a dry season. The mixed deciduous forest ends to the south and west where the weather is too dry to support the moisture-loving vegetation, and to the north where the climate becomes too cold and harsh and the growing season too short for the forest's plants and animals to produce offspring. The deciduous forest's leaf canopy is less dense than that of evergreen forests, so more sun gets through, allowing a larger number of plant species to grow on the ground below. That diversity provides a wide variety of habitats at many different levels within the forest. The result is a large selection of food and nesting sites for a great variety of animals.

All plants and animals in a community are intricately connected—some provide food, others eat the food. Each organism plays a special part in the community and each depends on many others. Living spaces fill with plants and animals suited to that spot. Some spaces are very small; some are large and include many habitats. It's fun to pick a small area and look very closely to see how many plants and animals are living together—as in this old tree stump.

It isn't neccessary to learn the scientific name of each animal and plant, but it can be fun. I have included Latin names in this book whenever possible, not because you must memorize them, but to make it easier for you to look up more information. Common names typically change from one area of the country to another, while Latin names remain the same.

The drawings, though not always to scale, make the interesting things easier to find. Add your own notes and drawings on the blank pages at the end of the book. Stop to listen, look, smell, touch—and enjoy.

ECOLOGICAL NICHE

Ecology is the study of the interrelations of plants and animals and their environment.

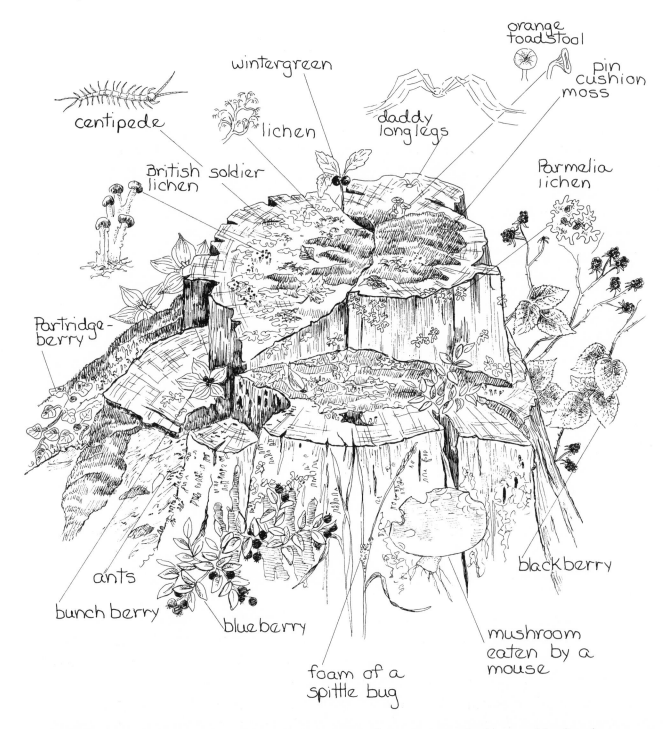

A niche is a small section of the environment that is particularly suitable for the organism in it. Several organisms may share a niche. It is interesting to study a small part of the environment to see how many plants and animals you can identify.

MAMMALS

BATS

Little Brown Bat (*Myotis lucifugus*)

The bat is our only flying mammal—its front legs are greatly modified to form wings (very different from a bird's wings). The bat's elongated fingers support the membrane that extends to the hind legs. The hind legs and tail act as supports as well.

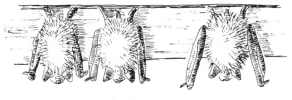

bats resting

Most bats eat insects, which they hunt by sonar detection. The bat makes high-pitched sounds, above the range of human hearing. The sounds echo and return to the bat's sensitive ears, revealing the size, shape, and location of nearby objects, including moving prey.

Many people think bats are dangerous and scary, but they are gentle, intelligent, and very interesting. Despite the myths, bats are not dirty (they spend a lot of time grooming), they will not get tangled in your hair, they do not attack people, their incidence of rabies is no greater than that of other animals.

The little brown bat, one of the most common bats, has narrow ears, a hairy face, and a dull brown coat that is lighter below. It roosts in buildings, trees, and caves and comes out at night to hunt for insects, usually near water. In cold weather, the little brown bat hibernates in caves and buildings.

little brown bat
(*Myotis lucifugus*)

3

BEAVER
(Castor canadensis)

The "busy" beaver, known for its beautiful fur, attracted trappers to the wilds of North America. The beaver's outer hairs are coarse, while the inner fur is fine and dense. An oily substance in glands at the base of the tail keeps the fur waterproof. The beaver is well adapted for spending a lot of time in the water. Its hind feet are webbed for swimming. When the animal submerges, its nostrils close. The scaly tail serves as an excellent rudder and paddle and also slaps the water to send an alarm. The beaver can submerge for up to fifteen minutes.

Beavers eat the inner bark and small twigs of a variety of trees (including alder, aspen, poplar, birch, and willow) and some water plants. Their incisor teeth grow constantly, and gnawing keeps the teeth worn down.

4

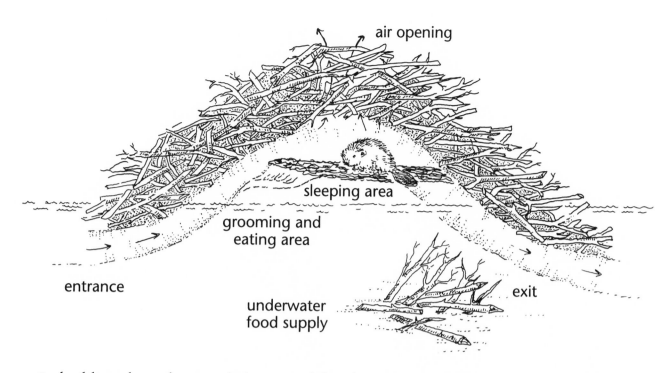

air opening

sleeping area

grooming and
eating area

entrance

underwater
food supply

exit

By building dams, beavers help control floods and create habitat for many other animals. Beavers first build a dam of mud, rocks, and sticks across a stream, creating a pond or lake. Then they build a house, or lodge, also of sticks and mud. The mud acts as cement and also insulates against winter's cold. The lodge is hollow, with room for sleeping as well as grooming and eating. Underwater tunnels allow the animals to enter and exit safely out of reach of predators. To allow for air circulation, the beavers leave spaces in the mud that cements the top of the lodge. A supply of sticks and branches cached near the lodge in the pond provides safe and easy meals during the winter. The whole family—parents, that year's kits, and the yearlings—spends the winter safe and warm in this snug lodge.

Their large, webbed hind feet make beavers powerful swimmers, able to travel up to 5 miles an hour in water. The two inner nails are split, allowing the animal to oil its fur and comb out lice.

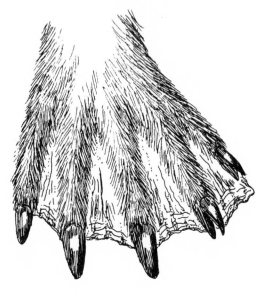

5

CHIPMUNK

Eastern Chipmunk (*Tamias striatus*)

The eastern chipmunk is reddish-brown with five black stripes on its back. Two stripes decorate the animal's sides; a white stripe runs down the chipmunk's back.

These busy and inquisitive little creatures eat insects, seeds, nuts, bulbs, flowers, and some small animals. They fiercely defend their home territory (about 100 square yards). The males compete aggressively for mates during the two yearly breeding periods.

The chipmunk's underground dens can be quite elaborate if used each year, containing tunnels 30 feet long, several rooms, and four or five entrances. The residents remove fresh soil from the entrances to fool enemies.

The animal's cheek pouches are flexible and rubbery. Lacking teeth between the front incisors and back grinders, the chipmunk stuffs food into the pouches—and reduces the number of food-gathering trips.

Chipmunks are not true hibernators. Instead of putting on body fat, they store food in their dens and awaken during the winter to eat. Once asleep, their heartbeat and breathing slow down and their body temperature falls.

EASTERN COTTONTAIL

(Sylvilagus floridanus)

The eastern cottontail is the most common rabbit in North America. It eats a variety of plant material, including bark, grass, herbs, twigs, and vegetables, and can become a pest to farmers and gardeners by destroying crops and trees.

Within hours of giving birth, a female can mate again. She can raise up to six litters a year. Although rabbits are very fertile, their death rate is also very high. Few live more than a year. They are an important prey animal to many predators, such as foxes, owls, bobcats, hawks, and crows.

Rabbits excrete two kinds of pellets. One is dry. The other is covered with mucus and contains valuable nutrients; these the rabbit eats and redigests.

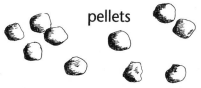

pellets

Hare or Rabbit?

Hares (in the genus *Lepus*) have long legs and ears, move about quickly, and use agility and speed to escape danger. They make no nest, and the young are born with fur and open eyes. In preparation for winter, their fur gradually turns white as the length of daylight decreases.

Rabbits are smaller and more stocky than hares. To escape danger they "freeze," hiding their white tails. Rabbits build nests of grass and fur. The young are born naked and blind, and need much care.

COYOTE
(Canis latrans)

For many of us, the howl of the coyote symbolizes freedom and the wildness of nature.

Coyotes started moving east from the western United States in the late 1800s. As settlers began cutting the Eastern forests, wolves moved out looking for larger prey, and the coyotes moved in to take the previous predator's place. They were able to increase their range partly because of the wide variety of foods they can eat, including fruit, grass, garbage, carrion, insects, frogs, skunks, rabbits, rodents, and birds. Coyotes can also adapt to many habitats, from forests to farms and even suburbia. The eastern coyote is larger than the western coyote. That may be a result of breeding with wolves or large dogs, or natural selection.

Since settlers first arrived in the East, bounties on coyotes have been used to shrink their populations—but their numbers haven't decreased. Intense hunting may have actually improved the breed by favoring the smart, fast, and adaptable individuals. Although coyotes occasionally kill a calf, sheep, or deer, some farmers are finding new respect for the animal's skill at killing large numbers of mice and rabbits.

WHITE-TAILED DEER

(Odocoileus virginianus)

These beautiful animals may be as numerous today as when settlers first arrived in North America. White-tailed deer thrive on the edges of farms, woodlots, and wetlands, areas that provide a variety of food and cover. Deer browse on buds, leaves, and the twigs of woody plants as well as acorns and some farm crops. They are the most important big-game animal of eastern North America.

Fawns have no scent for the first three or four days of life and their beautiful spotted coat blends in with the vegetation. By lying perfectly still in the grass among the shadows and sunlight, a fawn usually remains unseen by predators.

Male deer, called bucks, grow antlers made of solid bone each year. Their antlers display the animal's dominance and sexual attractiveness and are sometimes used to fight off rivals. The antler's size and shape are a result of nutrition, not age. A layer of fuzzy skin, called velvet, containing blood vessels and nerve endings covers and nourishes the antlers as they grow. In late summer growth stops, and the outer skin hardens. Over the next month, males rub off the velvet by attacking saplings and twigs with their antlers, a process that sometimes leaves blood stains on the antlers. November heralds the breeding season, or rut, during which time bucks may behave wildly. After breeding, the shedding process begins, and the antlers fall off sometime between late fall and early spring. Mice, chipmunks, and porcupines eat the antlers, which contain nutritious minerals, calcium, and salt. Some bucks, weakened by growing the large antlers and fighting other deer, may not make it through the winter.

The prominent tail gives the "white-tail" its name. When a deer is alarmed, the tail flips up and fluffs out, providing a large warning signal to other deer.

RED FOX

(Vulpes vulpes)

The beautiful little fox is known for its intelligence and craftiness—recognized in our adjective "foxy." That intelligence has helped the red fox become our most widespread wild dog. Able to live in open forests, fields, brushland, and even fairly populated areas, they eat a wide variety of food—fruit, berries, corn, worms, insects, eggs, birds, carrion, rodents, and other small mammals.

The color of the silky pelt varies from the usual red to silver, brown, and black even within the same litter. In winter, the fur provides a warm insulating coat. Under the long outer hair lies a thick undercoat that traps air for warmth. The fox's fluffy tail, which can cover its nose, and the furred foot pads help keep it snug in cold weather.

Red foxes raise their four to eight pups in a den equipped with several exits for safety. If they feel threatened, the parents will move their pups to another den. Although they can dig their own, foxes prefer to use another animal's existing burrow.

11

MICE AND VOLES

(family Cricetidae)

Mice have large ears and eyes, long tails, and pointed faces.

The deer mouse is one of the most widely distributed mice. Even though there are sixty kinds of deer mice, you don't often see them—they are small, fast, and secretive. Like its namesake, the deer, this mouse varies from grayish to reddish brown above and white below. Active all year, the deer mouse spends much of its time above ground and nests almost anywhere—in logs, stumps, sheds, old bird nests, niches in walls, and unused burrows. Deer mice eat seeds, nuts, berries, insects, bark, and buds.

The white-footed mouse (*Peromyscus leucopus*) is very similar but not as widely distributed.

deer mouse
(*Peromyscus maniculatus*)

Voles have small ears and eyes, short tails, and blunt faces. They spend most of their time under cover in tunnels formed in grass or leaves. Voles may be one of the most common mammals and are a major source of food for predatory birds and mammals.

Meadow voles, the most common voles, remain active all year. Their long, soft fur varies from gray to dark brown. When the snow melts, you can see their runways through the field grass. Their nests look like balls of grass. They leave their droppings at the tunnel crossings, whereas mice leave them in their nests. Under cover of snow, they gnaw the bark off fruit trees, causing great damage.

meadow vole
(*Microtus pennsylvanicus*)

MOLES

Star-Nosed Mole (*Condylura cristata*)

Moles are small (the body is 4 to 5 inches long) and have soft, velvety, gray fur. Their fur does not lie in any one direction, so when they are underground dirt does not collect under the fur. Moles have tiny eyes (some covered with thin skin) and poor eyesight.

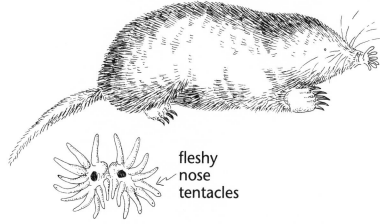

They hear well but lack external ears. The mole's snout sports sensitive whiskers and many nerve endings. Their well-developed sense of touch proves useful underground in the dark. Moles eat earthworms and insects, and sometimes consume three times their weight in 24 hours.

fleshy nose tentacles

The star-nosed mole has 22 fleshy, fingerlike projections on its nose. These very sensitive nose tentacles help the animal find its prey. In late winter and early spring, the mole's tail thickens with fat stored for the breeding season. The star-nosed mole spends more time above ground than other moles.

Moles spend most of their lives underground, digging elaborate tunnels. They are well adapted for that: their strong front legs and shoulder girdle support powerful muscles. Their huge paws, each with five claws, face outward and serve as shovels to scoop away the soil. Sometimes moles dig through large volumes of dirt in 24 hours. They raise their young in deep tunnels.

mole tunnel seen from above ground

13

PORCUPINE

(Erethizon dorsatum)

These slow-moving animals are known for being covered by about 30,000 quills. Muscles that control each quill enable the porcupine to raise them in the face of danger. If attacked, the porcupine will whip its tail back and forth, causing some quills to fly at the attacker. The porcupine does not "shoot" quills at an enemy; they merely fall out because they are loosely attached. New ones soon grow in.

The quill's sharp tip has tiny fishhooklike barbs that make it very hard to pull it out of the skin. It may help to cut the tip, which releases air pressure inside. If the quills aren't removed they can work in deeper and even cause death.

Although porcupines have a keen sense of smell and very sensitive whiskers, their sight and hearing are poor. A porcupine may waddle up very close before seeing you.

This animal's favorite summer foods include clover, dandelions, and alfalfa. In winter, they eat the inner bark of trees such as willow and aspen. Special pads on their feet keep them from slipping when climbing trees; large incisors allow them to strip the bark; and 25 feet of intestine equipped with special bacteria aid digestion. Beavers crave salt and often annoy humans by eating objects soaked in sweat, such as tool handles, gloves, boots, and ropes.

RACCOON

(Procyon lotor)

Recognize the mischievous raccoon by its black mask and ringed tail.

Raccoons eat almost anything—fish, crayfish, insects, rodents, fruit, nuts, corn, garbage, and carrion. Their sharp-clawed paws are skillful and sensitive. Although they sometimes appear to wash their food, they are just catching or feeling for prey in the water.

You may see raccoons roaming at night—especially near garbage cans. They sleep during the day and den in hollow trees, under rocks, in old animal dens, and even in garages and attics. These intelligent animals easily adapt to living near people.

15

SHREWS

(family Soricidae)

Although the shrew is the smallest mammal, it can be one of the fiercest. Shrews eat all kinds of insects, snails, earthworms, snakes, salamanders, mice, and even other shrews. These creatures are constantly active, looking for food. Because of their small size and high metabolic rate, they must eat a lot or risk starvation. Sometimes a shrew will eat several times its own body weight in food in 24 hours. Shrews breathe ten times for every human breath, and their heart beats 700 to 1,200 times a minute.

The northern short-tailed shrew has venom in its saliva to help paralyze its prey. This poison usually affects humans only mildly. The platypus is the only other poisonous mammal.

northern short-tailed shrew
(*Blarina brevicauda*)

Shrews are the size of mice or smaller. Their small, beady eyes are not covered with skin (they have no lids), and their ears usually lie concealed within their fur. The shrew's vision is poor, but its hearing and smell are acute. Though they resemble mice and moles, shrews have five toes on each foot (most mice have four toes on the front feet), and their feet are not shaped for digging like a mole's. Their teeth are pigmented reddish-brown, making a shrew's skull easy to pick out in owl pellets. To locate prey, shrews bounce high-pitched squeals off objects and listen for the echoes.

STRIPED SKUNK

(Mephitis mephitis)

This pretty black and white mammal is infamous for spraying a smelly liquid from scent glands under its tail. When a skunk feels threatened it gives a warning by hissing, stamping its feet, arching its back, and raising its tail. Then watch out! Strong muscles squeeze the glands that shoot the musky liquid up to 16 feet away. The odor travels much farther on the wind. The spray temporarily blinds the victim, burns the skin, and upsets the stomach. Young skunks can spray at as early as seven weeks of age. The glands replace the fluid in about a week. Tomato juice or vinegar will help cut the smell on a sprayed family pet—or you.

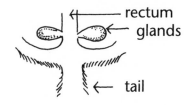

rectum
glands
tail

If left alone, skunks are harmless and peaceful and can make nice pets (when de-scented). They actually help humans by eating many insect and rodent pests.

GRAY SQUIRREL

(Sciurus carolinensis)

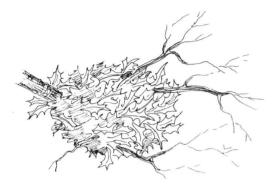

The gray squirrel spends most of its time in the upper branches of trees, using its bushy tail for balance and steering. When dropping from high branches, squirrels use their tail as a parachute and a brake.

Gray squirrels successfully adapt to many environments, including cities. They are active all winter. In warm weather, gray squirrels make their home in a nest of leaves; a den in a tree becomes their winter home.

Black squirrels are just a color phase of the gray squirrel. Albinos also exist.

Gray squirrels eat nuts, tree buds and shoots, fruit, seeds, and sometimes insects, mushrooms, small birds, and bird eggs. These creatures hide and store nuts all over, then locate them later by scent. Those missed often sprout and become trees.

TRACKS (not to scale)

Although you may not see wild animals during a hike, you will likely discover their tracks. The following are typical prints and trail patterns.

1. Tracks in a straight line

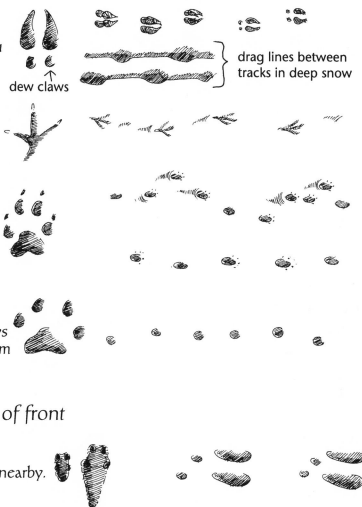

Deer (and other hooved animals)
Often the hind feet are placed in the print of the front feet. In deep snow, you may see drag marks between tracks.

dew claws

drag lines between tracks in deep snow

Birds
Game birds and those that spend a lot of time on the ground tend to walk.

Dog Family
Print is oval with four toes and claws. The trail of the common dog is meandering, and the feet drag. A wild dog's trail is cautiously straight.

Cat Family
Print is roundish with four toes. The claws do not show. The print size increases from domestic cat to bobcat to lynx.

2. Leaping–hind feet print ahead of front

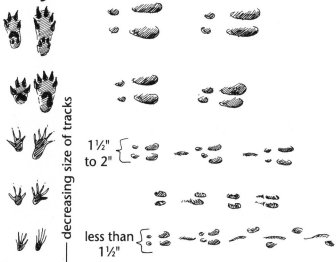

Rabbit
Typical leaping pattern, droppings often nearby.

Gray Squirrel
Similar to rabbit prints but smaller.

Eastern Chipmunk
(Hibernates in winter)

Deer Mouse
Sometimes the tail drags.

Meadow Vole
Patterns vary greatly, often tunnel under snow.

Shrew
Pattern varies greatly from walking to leaping, sometimes tail drags.

decreasing size of tracks

1½" to 2"

less than 1½"

19

3. Evenly spaced pairs or groups

Birds
Birds that spend most of their time in trees hop on the ground.

Short-tailed weasel
Tunnels in snow, hind feet usually land in tracks of front feet.

Mink
Look for tracks near water, also tunnels in snow.

Skunk
Digs holes in search of insects.

Otter
Look for tracks near water, may be marks of a sliding body.

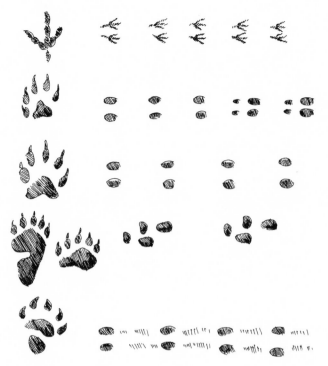

4. Waddling (heavyset, wide straddle)

Muskrat
Look for tracks near water, tail sometimes drags.

Opossum
Distinctive track with large, thumblike toe.

Raccoon
Tracks look like small human feet and hands.

Porcupine
Pigeon-toed prints with brush marks from quills.

Beaver
Hind foot webbed, tail drag may cover tracks.

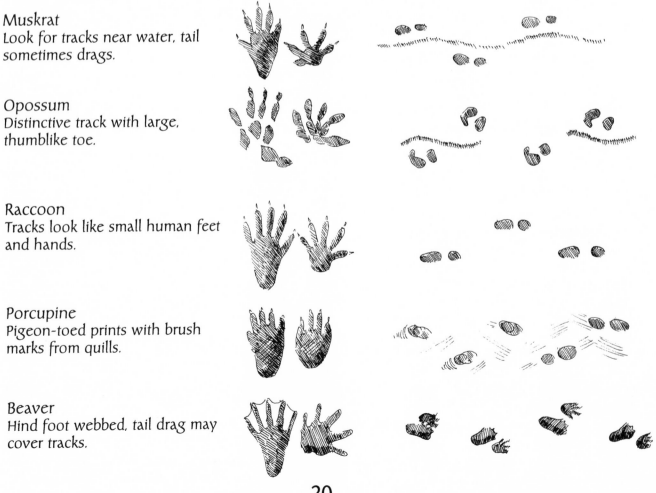

20

It's fun to try to read the stories told by tracks and other clues. You may not be able to identify the animal, but you can look for other facts—was the animal walking, running, eating, being chased?

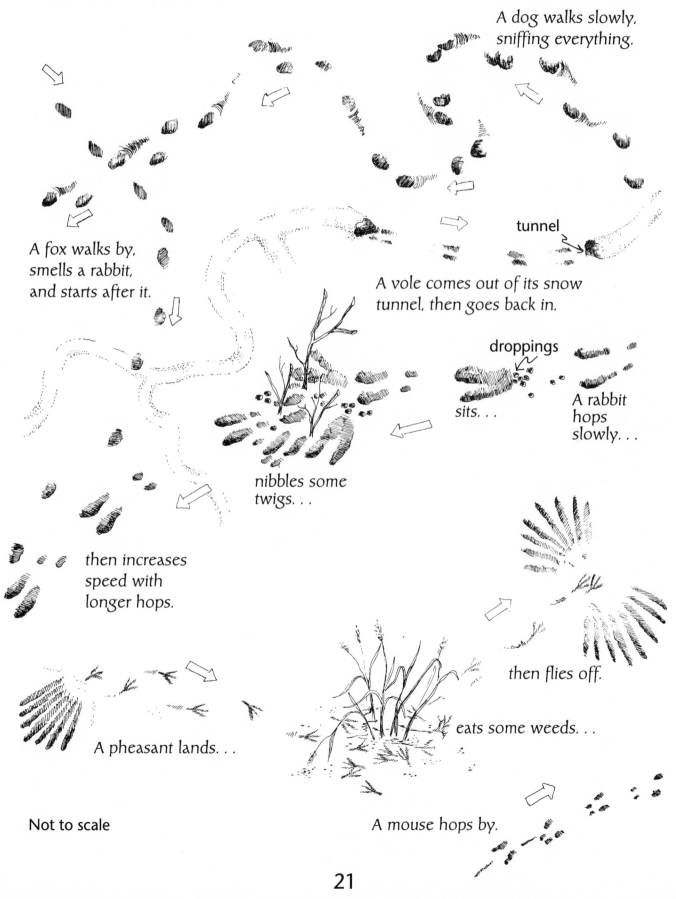

A dog walks slowly, sniffing everything.

A fox walks by, smells a rabbit, and starts after it.

tunnel

A vole comes out of its snow tunnel, then goes back in.

droppings

sits. . .

A rabbit hops slowly. . .

nibbles some twigs. . .

then increases speed with longer hops.

then flies off.

A pheasant lands. . .

eats some weeds. . .

A mouse hops by.

Not to scale

NATURE'S CLUES

Typically you will find evidence of wildlife (tracks, droppings, food remains, chewed twigs, scent, hair, feathers) rather than the bird or mammal itself. By analyzing these clues, you can find out what the animal ate, where it went, and other interesting facts.

sapsucker holes

spruce bark beetle tunnels

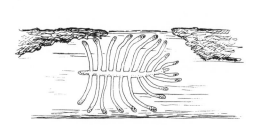

woodpecker holes

These birds bore holes in tree bark and use their brush-like tongues to suck up the sap. Sapsuckers also come back to eat the insects that are attracted to the sap.

The female beetle bores a central egg tunnel. After hatching, the larvae bore their own side tunnels.

Woodpeckers chisel holes in search of insects.

Acorns opened by a

| bird | squirrel | mouse | vole |

 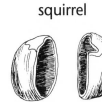

To open a nut, a bird hammers on it with its beak, leaving a jagged opening. A squirrel, after making a hole in the top, inserts its lower teeth and uses them as a lever to split the nut. A mouse gnaws on the far side of the nut, and its incisors leave marks on the outside of the hole. A vole gnaws the near side, leaving teeth marks on the inside of the hole.

Voles usually move about in tunnels. They leave their droppings at tunnel intersections; mice deposit their droppings in their nest.

vole tunnels under the snow

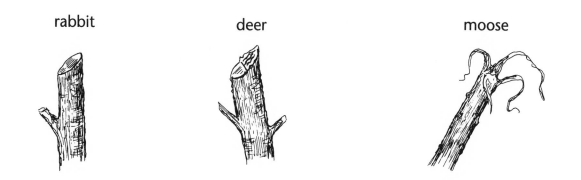

rabbit

deer

moose

A rabbit uses its sharp upper and lower teeth when nibbling a twig. That leaves a smooth cut on the remaining twig. A deer has no upper incisors and so leaves the twig part smooth and part ragged. A moose holds the branch with its tongue, then pulls it as its lower teeth cut. That leaves the twig ragged.

squirrel midden

seeds eaten by a mouse

Squirrels eat the seeds of conifers and leave the wings in a large pile called a midden. Mice also eat conifer seeds but scatter them around.

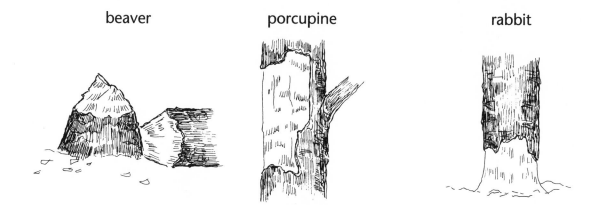

beaver

porcupine

rabbit

Teeth marks on felled trees are the marks of beavers. Porcupines feed on the inner bark, usually high in the tree, never penetrating the wood. Rabbits gnaw bark from the bottom of the tree. Look for the four furrows made by the upper incisors.

Animal tracks and owl pellets are described in their own sections.

WINTER SURVIVAL

With the coming of winter's cold and snow, the food supply of many animals dwindles or disappears. Creatures either have to leave the area or adapt to the harsh conditions. Some animals adapt by hibernating. During hibernation, mammals become inactive and need little food. Body temperature drops until it almost matches that of the surrounding environment. Heartbeat and breathing slow dramatically. The animals are not sensitive to touch. The warming spring temperatures finally arouse them. Mammals that are true hibernators include the woodchuck, ground squirrel, jumping mouse, and certain bats.

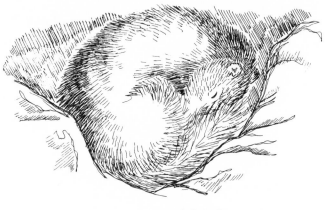

woodchuck

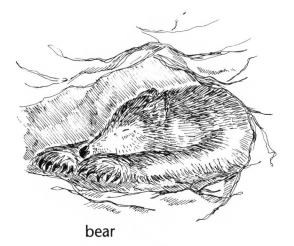

bear

Some mammals go into a deep sleep that is not hibernation. It is called dormancy. Their temperature and metabolism slow somewhat, but they remain sensitive to touch and wake up occasionally to feed. Mammals that go dormant during winter include the bear, opossum, skunk, raccoon, and badger.

Most birds migrate to escape the cold winters. Birds that do stay feed on seeds, berries, hibernating insects, and other animals. To keep warm, birds huddle or fluff their feathers to create insulating air spaces.

fluffed bird

Cold-blooded reptiles and amphibians go into a stupor. Their body temperature drops to near freezing, and their heartbeat becomes very slow. Below 40 degrees F, they typically absorb oxygen from the water through their skin. Glycerol in the bodies of reptiles and amphibians acts as a natural antifreeze to protect the organs. Snakes curl together in large numbers in underground burrows. Many frogs and turtles bury themselves in the mud.

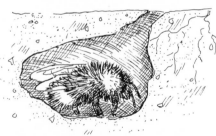

Some fish species, such as the yellow bullhead, bury themselves in the mud. Others, including the yellow perch, hover almost motionless just off the bottom.

While monarch butterflies migrate south for the winter, many other insects die. Some, however, survive. These adults, pupae, or eggs hibernate, concealed underground in plant debris, tree branches, or pond bottoms.

The adult mourning cloak takes refuge in cracks of tree trunks and branches.

Queen bumblebees hibernate in underground holes.

Praying mantis eggs spend the winter in a hard case attached to a branch or twig.

Isabelle moths hibernate in plant debris as woolly caterpillars, the larval form of the moth.

Katydid eggs survive the winter on leaves and twigs.

Adult water boatsmen cling to underwater stems all winter.

BIRDS

BLACK-CAPPED CHICKADEE

(Parus atricapillus)

You can easily recognize the cheerful little chickadee by its black cap and bib. In summer, the chickadee eats insects, seeds, spiders, and berries and other fruit. During winter, it searches for cocoons, insect eggs, and dormant insects. The black-capped chickadee is one of the first visitors to winter feeding stations.

Both males and females utter the nasal "chick-a-dee" call. Males also voice a clear, whistling "chick-a-dee" and a territorial "fee-bee." Listen for "chit-chit-chit" when two males are chasing each other.

This bird's acrobatics are fun to watch. They easily hang upside while looking for food.

Inquisitive chickadees may accept food right from your hand. Try holding sunflower seeds, and see if chickadees will come to you. The birds will carry off the seeds one at a time, hold them with their feet, and peck them open.

29

COMMON CROW

(Corvus brachyrhynchos)

The common crow, a deep, glossy black, grows to be 17 to 21 inches tall. The crow builds its large platform nest in the top of a tree.

Crows are intelligent and adaptable. Some can imitate other birdcalls, imitate human words or laughter, whistle, solve puzzles, and hide objects.

The crow's extremely varied diet includes small mammals, large quantities of insects, bird eggs, carrion, weed seeds, grain waste, fruits, reptiles, and crustaceans. These birds have been known to destroy some crops, but they also eat large quantities of harmful insects, such as grasshoppers and cutworms.

During the winter, crows gather, sometimes by the thousands, in communal roosts at night. During the day small groups fly off to search for food.

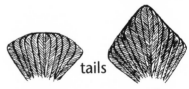

tails

crow   raven

The raven resembles the crow but is much larger (up to 27 inches tall). The raven's call is a deep croaking "wonk wonk," while the crow's call is "caw caw." The raven's tail is wedge-shaped; the crow's tail is fanlike. The raven has shaggy throat feathers and a stout bill.

raven

30

HERRING GULL

(Larus argentatus)

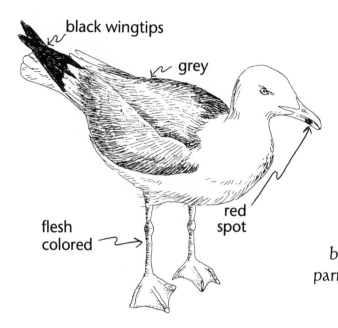

black wingtips

grey

red spot

flesh colored

Often called seagulls, herring gulls don't actually venture far out to sea. They typically live far inland near farms and fields as often as near beaches and coasts. Gulls are scavengers, feeding on a variety of food but primarily dead fish and garbage. Adult plumage takes three to four years to develop. Until then the birds are a mottled brown. The young instinctively peck at the bright red spot on the parent's bill. The adult responds by regurgitating partially digested food for them.

Like owls, gulls regurgitate undigested remains in pellets. Look for small pieces of shell, fish bones, and plant debris where you see gulls.

Herring gulls are strong fliers. They swim well on top of the water, but they are poor divers.

Be careful not to confuse gulls with the slim, streamlined terns. Terns dive headfirst for their prey but rarely swim on the surface because their feet are not adapted for swimming.

pellet

tern

HUMMINGBIRD

Ruby-Throated Hummingbird (*Archilochus colubris*)

Of the more than 300 hummingbird species, the 3-inch-tall ruby-throated is the only one that lives in the eastern United States and Canada. The male has a beautifully iridescent red throat and a forked tail; the female lacks the red on the throat and has a blunt tail with white spots. Ruby-throated hummingbirds feed on insects, spiders, and nectar (especially from red, tubular flowers). This bird's long tongue works like a suction pump to suck the nectar out of flowers. The hummer uses so much energy that it may need to eat fifty to sixty times in a day. The bird's daily sugar intake may equal half of its weight.

The female makes a tiny nest (1½ inches in diameter) lined with plant down and lichens anchored with spider silk.

Ruby-throated hummingbirds are the only birds that can hover or fly backward. To hover, the bird beats its wings in a figure 8 about 50 times per second. Top forward speed can reach 30 miles per hour. The bird's wing muscles are enormous compared to its size. Hummingbirds depend so much on flying that they can barely walk on their underdeveloped legs. These tiny birds migrate over 2,000 miles to Mexico, Panama, and the Gulf States.

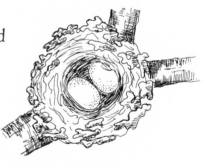

hovering in a figure 8

KILLDEER

(Charadrius vociferous)

The killdeer has a white breast and belly, a golden rump, and two black breast bands. The bird calls a loud "kill-deeah" or sometimes a mournful "dee-ee, dee, dee, dee." The nest is a shallow depression on rocky or sandy ground. The four speckled eggs, large for the size of the bird and containing a large yolk sac, are incubated for 24 to 26 days. These factors enable the young to be born well developed and soon able to take care of themselves.

When the nest is threatened, one of the parents will spread its tail to show a bright rusty rump. Then it drags a wing and flutters along, as if it were wounded. That usually leads attackers away from eggs or young.

GREAT HORNED OWL

(Bubo virginianus)

The great horned, known for its large earlike feather tufts, is one of North America's largest owls. They eat a variety of animals, including beetles, frogs, rats, squirrels, birds, and even skunks and porcupines. The owl's sharp beak and talons help it hold and tear apart its prey.

The great horned owl's eyes are set in the front of its head, giving it a very human look. This eye placement also gives the owl some three-dimensional vision—similar to human vision—which is critical in judging size and distance. Because the eyes are fixed in their sockets, the owl must swivel its head around to see to the side.

These birds of the night are well adapted to hunting in the dark. Their pupils open very wide to let in light, and the retina is packed with receptors sensitive to low light levels. The owl's flight feathers have fringed edges that break the air flow and allow for silent flight.

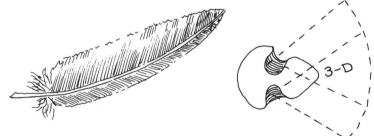

Owls have keen hearing. Facial feathers direct sound waves to the ear openings, which are located asymmetrically on the head. By catching the sounds at slightly different times, the bird can pinpoint its prey.

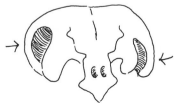

OWL PELLETS

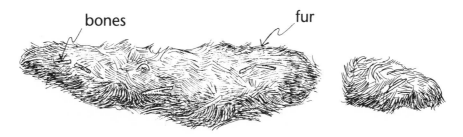

bones fur

An owl cannot digest bones, feathers, or fur. Those materials are slowly compacted in the bird's gizzard and then regurgitated as a mucus-covered pellet that quickly dries. Look for pellets under an owl's nest. By carefully pulling apart a pellet, you will find clues to the owl's diet. Owl pellets consist mostly of the remains (hair, skulls and other bones, beaks, and feet) of shrews, meadow voles, mice, and birds.

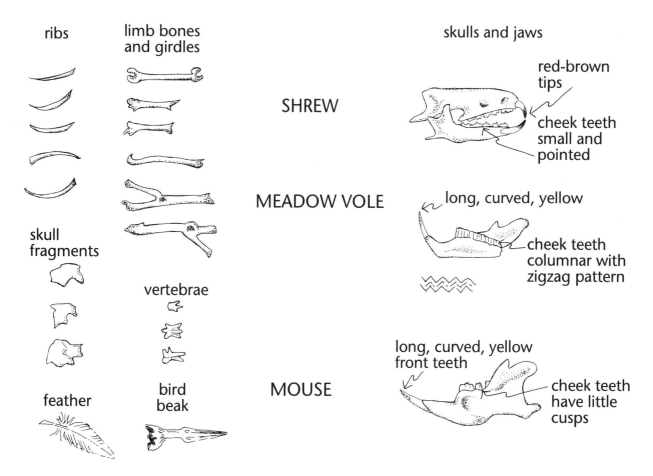

ribs limb bones and girdles skulls and jaws

SHREW

red-brown tips

cheek teeth small and pointed

skull fragments

vertebrae

MEADOW VOLE

long, curved, yellow

cheek teeth columnar with zigzag pattern

long, curved, yellow front teeth

feather bird beak MOUSE

cheek teeth have little cusps

Other birds also leave pellets. Hawks can digest bones, so their pellets contain fur, feathers, claws, and beak coverings, and are more loosely constructed than owl pellets. Crow pellets contain a lot of plant material. Gull pellets contain sea shells, insects, bones, and plant material. Fox droppings resemble pellets but are pointed at both ends.

ROBIN

(Turdus migratorius)

When early settlers came to North America, they were homesick for familiar birds, so they named the robin after their red-breasted European robin, a bird not found in North America.

Everyone has probably found a robin's nest made of mud and grass. To form the nest's inner mud cup, the bird turns its body around and around inside the nest. The robin lines its nest with feathers and grass.

If you watch robins hunting for food on the lawn, you may think they are listening for earthworms. The birds don't have a good sense of smell or hearing, however, and they are actually looking for worms by cocking their head.

If you find a baby robin alone, it is best to leave it be. The young bird is probably not an orphan but has just left the nest temporarily, and the parents are usually nearby. Young robins, like many members of the thrush family, have spotted breasts that become a beautiful brick red when they become adults.

HOUSE SPARROW

(Passer domesticus)

male

The house sparrow, also called
English sparrow, is native to Eurasia and
North Africa. It belongs in a different family
(weaver finch) than our native sparrows. In
1850, a few house sparrows were released in New York City's Central Park to control
canker worms. They succeeded too well and became a problem. Because they are so
aggressive and quarrelsome, house sparrows chase many native birds from the best
nesting sites, tear up nests, destroy eggs and young, and compete for food. Conse-
quently, populations of bluebirds, martins, wrens, and other songbirds have decreased.

female

BARN SWALLOW

(Hirundo rustica)

The swallow is built for fast flight and long migrations. Its long, narrow, swept-back wings enable it to spend much of the day catching insects on the wing. Swallows eat large numbers of mosquitoes and flies.

The birds originally attached their nests to tree trunks and rocky ledges. With the westward movement of farmers, barn swallows began to nest in the rafters and ledges of barns and outbuildings as well.

Swallows build their nests with beakfuls of mud pellets. They add layers of straw between the mud for strength and line the inside of the nest with feathers and hair.

DOWNY WOODPECKER

(Picoides pubescens)

The little downy woodpecker is one of the most common and tamest woodpeckers in the East. The downy resembles the hairy woodpecker, but the downy is smaller, with a much smaller bill and black bars on the white outer tail feathers. In both species, the male has a red patch on the back of the head.

Special adaptations allow the woodpecker to peck with its bill while securely gripping a tree trunk. Powerful neck muscles and a chisel-shaped bill help the bird bore wood in search of insects and larvae. The bone of the skull is very strong and contains air spaces that absorb the shock of hammering.

red patch

stiff tail

The woodpecker's feet provide excellent grip on bark, with the toes arranged two forward and two backward rather than the usual three forward and one backward.

Stiff tail feathers brace the bird's body against the tree trunk while the woodpecker pounds away.

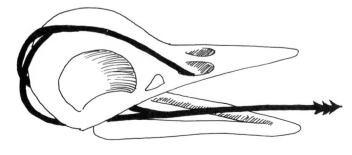

The tongue, attached at the front of the skull, curves over the top of the skull and into the mouth. A downy woodpecker can shoot its tongue out twice the length of its head to nab food. The tip of the tongue is sticky with pointed bristles that catch insects and larvae.

BIRD NESTS

Most nest-building birds hatch young that are blind, naked, and helpless for several weeks. Such birds are called altricial. The hatchlings' survival depends on the protection and concealment of their nests. The nests incubate the young, moderating temperature and moisture. Fall and early winter are the best time to find nests—after the inhabitants have abandoned them and before winter destroys them. Most birds build new nests each year; birds of prey repair their old ones.

Ninety percent of the nests found in the northeastern United States and adjacent Canada are built by catbirds, chipping sparrows, goldfinches, northern orioles, redstarts, robins, song sparrows, red-eyed vireos, and yellow warblers.

Ground Nesters

The newly hatched young of some ground-nesting birds, including killdeer, nighthawk, woodcock, and piping plover, are precocial (able to run and feed almost immediately). At birth they are covered with down and their eyes are open. Their nest may be only a slight depression in the ground. Typically, one must see the adults or eggs to identify the nest. Some bird species build nests on or near the ground but hatch young that are not precocial—for example, bobolinks, field sparrows, veeries, and song sparrows.

killdeer depression on the ground

Hole Dwellers

woodpecker hole

Woodpeckers excavate new holes in trees for their nests each year. The size of the hole depends on the size of the bird. Bluebirds, chickadees, house sparrows, and nuthatches reuse woodpecker excavations for their own nests, often lining them with grass, sticks, or feathers. If holes look old, with healed edges, other bird species may be using them.

Nests

Some nests are distinctive and easy to identify.

Hummingbird
A very small cup (less than 1½ inches in diameter) cup made of plant fibers, down, and lichens, all attached with spider silk.

Northern Oriole
A hanging basket of intricately woven fibers, string, hair, and bark strips.

Chimney Swift
A shallow cup of sticks glued together with saliva. Look for them in chimneys, silos, barns, and hollow trees.

Barn Swallow
Formed of layers of mud and straw plastered to building beams.

Similar Cuplike Nests

These nests are common but hard to identify.

Robin
This nest has an inner layer of mud and a grass lining. The wood thrush, phoebe, and grackle make similar nests.

Goldfinch
A small, neat cup formed of thistle or cattail down. Yellow warbler and redstart nests are similar but lack down.

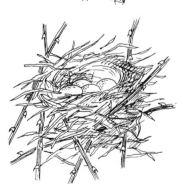

Catbird
This is a bulky nest, built in briars and thickets and made of twigs and rootlets. Blue jay and brown thrasher nests are similar.

Red-Winged Blackbird
Deeply hollow and built in reeds, rushes, and cattails. The marsh wren's nest is similar but more spherical.

You will find many more interesting nests well illustrated and described in field guides to bird nests.

REPTILES

GARTER SNAKE

(Thamnophis sirtalis)

This harmless creature is one of the most common snakes in North America. It prefers damp places, such as ditches, marshes, moist fields, and woods. Garter snakes eat toads, frogs, earthworms, salamanders, and sometimes mice, fish, and dead birds. The young, born live from June to August, take about two years to mature. In the north, garter snakes hibernate in large groups. Those in the south remain active all year. When captured, these snakes may eject an unpleasant-smelling fluid from their vent glands.

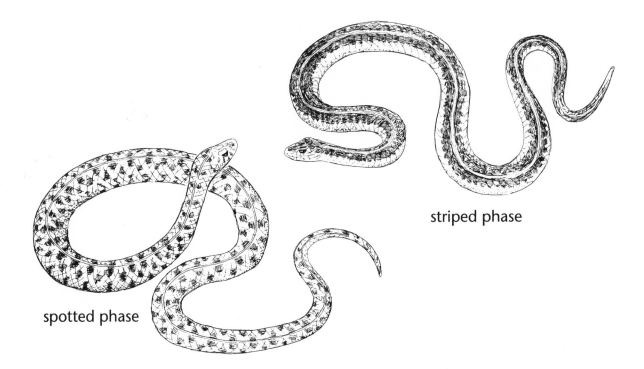

striped phase

spotted phase

The garter snake's coloration, markings, and patterns vary widely among the many subspecies. They usually have three (though sometimes two) yellow stripes (which may also be brown, green, or bluish). A dark area between the stripes may be spotted.

Like all snakes, this reptile molts periodically. Before it molts the snake's eyes cloud over, and the animal hides under logs, rocks, and vegetation. By rubbing against rough surfaces, the snake pulls off the old skin. Watch for the tissue-thin molted skin with its scalelike impressions.

PAINTED TURTLE

(Chrysemys picta)

Look for the eastern painted turtle, one of the most common water turtles, sunbathing on logs and rocks.

This turtle gets its name from the painted look of the red and yellow markings on its carapace, or top shell. Turtles lack teeth but have a hard beak with sharp ridges. The male is usually smaller than the female and has a concave plastron, or bottom shell. That makes it easier for him to mount the female for mating. During courtship, the male waves its long front claws in front of the female.

carapace (olive to black)

plastron (yellow)

red and yellow markings

The female lays 5 to 8 soft, rubbery white eggs in a hole dug near a pond, then covers them with soil and leaves. Sunlight warming the soil incubates the eggs. Turtles lack sex chromosomes, so the nest temperature determines the sex of the young. If the eggs are cool, they hatch as males. If they are warm, they hatch as females. The young dig themselves out and survive for a few days by eating their yolk sacs, then they begin to hunt for themselves. Painted turtles eat water plants, insects, and small animals. Birds, frogs, and fish prey on the young turtles; skunks, raccoons, and fox eat turtle eggs.

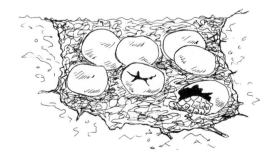

AMPHIBIANS

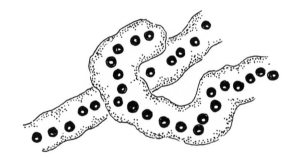

FROGS

Pickerel Frog
(Rana palustris)
size: 1¾" to 3¼"

This frog has dark, square spots on its back and yellow-orange shading on the belly and underside of the legs. The pickerel frog gives off a skin secretion that burns and irritates a predator's mouth, making the hunter spit out the frog. The toxic secretion can also kill other frogs in the same terrarium. Its call is a low, short snore or croak. In summer you may find it far from water, searching for insects, worms, and spiders in field grass.

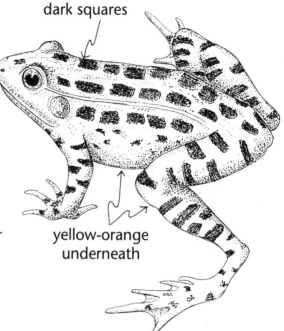

dark squares

yellow-orange underneath

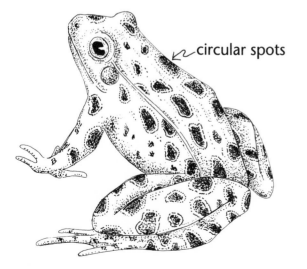

circular spots

Leopard Frog
(Rana pipiens)
size: 2" to 5"

The leopard frog sports circular spots with light borders. The underside of its legs are white. In summer, it may wander quite far from water in search of insects, worms, and spiders. Its call is a rattling snore with clacking grunts.

Spring Peeper
(Hyla crucifer)
size: ¾" to 1¼"

The spring peeper, the size of a penny, is one of our smallest frogs. A dark gray-brown X marks its light tan or gray back, and its toes have sticky disks for climbing. The peeper's call is a high, bell-like sound that carries a long distance.

Wood Frog
(Rana sylvatica)
size: 1¼" to 3¼"

Recognize the wood frog by the dark mask through its eye, ending behind the eardrum. This frog's body is usually several shades of brown. Wood frogs inhabit woodlands and utter a short, hoarse, quacklike call.

Gray Tree Frog
(Hyla versicolor)
size: 1¼" to 2¼"

The gray tree frog can change color from gray to brown to green. It has an irregular star on its back, is orange on the underside of its hind legs, and has a light spot under its eye. In summer, gray tree frogs can be found in tree tops and far from water. Listen for the call, a short birdlike trill.

Bullfrog
(Rana catesbeiana)
size: 3⅛" to 8"

Our largest frog, at up to 8 inches long, the bullfrog is nearly all green. The fourth toe of the hind foot protrudes beyond the webbing of the foot. The bullfrog lives in or close to the water all its life. The male bullfrog's booming call, "jug-o-rum," fills the night air during the breeding season.

Green Frog
(Rana clamitans)
size: 2" to 4"

This frog is green to brown, usually with dark blotches. Its "tchung" call sounds like the dull twang of a loose banjo string. The male's throat is yellowish white; the female's is white. The green tree frog has a pair of wrinkles, one on each side, running down its back.

51

EASTERN NEWT

(Notophthalmus viridescens)

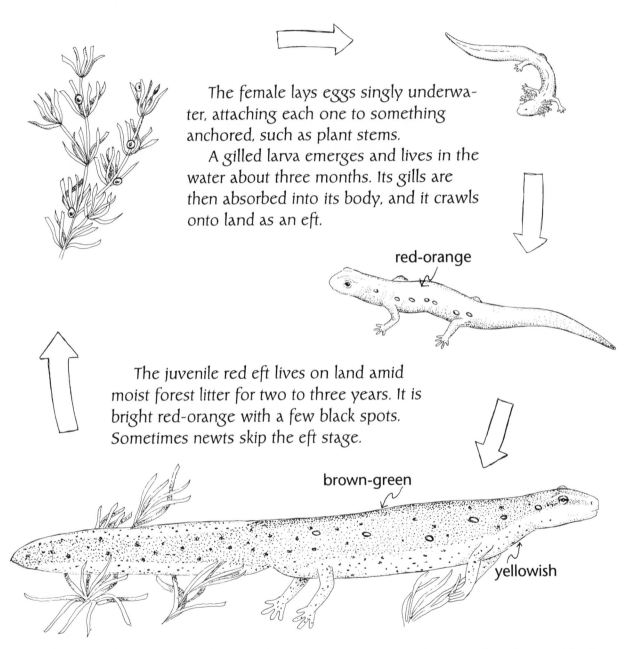

The female lays eggs singly underwater, attaching each one to something anchored, such as plant stems.

A gilled larva emerges and lives in the water about three months. Its gills are then absorbed into its body, and it crawls onto land as an eft.

red-orange

The juvenile red eft lives on land amid moist forest litter for two to three years. It is bright red-orange with a few black spots. Sometimes newts skip the eft stage.

brown-green

yellowish

The adult, brownish green above and yellowish below with several dark spots both above and below, returns to the water to live. The tail is shaped like a keel to aid in swimming. The adult eastern newt eats small aquatic animals, eggs, and large insects. The larvae, living on land, eat similar but smaller insects and animals found in moist vegetation.

AMERICAN TOAD

(Bufo americanus)

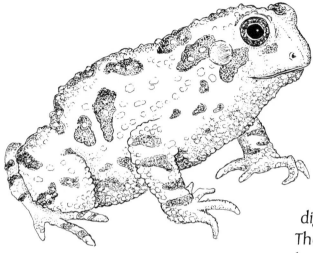

The common toad lives in cool, damp woods and fields. A toad spends more time out of water than a frog. The toad's lungs are more efficient. Toads hop rather than jump. Toads do not cause warts, but if they are frightened their skin glands can ooze a milky juice that burns and irritates their enemy's eyes and mouth, causing the predator to spit out the toad. Toads can also puff themselves up to scare enemies, or dig themselves backward into the dirt to hide. The toad's call is a musical trill up to 30 seconds long.

The long, sticky tongue, attached to the front of the toad's mouth, moves extremely fast to catch insects. Toads eat hundreds of harmful garden insects, usually at night.

Females lay up to 15,000 eggs in long strings.

Adults return to the water to mate.

The tadpole emerges with external gills and a long tail.

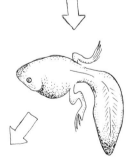

As the tadpole develops hind legs and then front legs, its tail shrinks. It loses its gills as lungs develop. The nibbling mouth changes to a wide, snapping mouth.

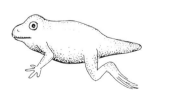

Tadpoles eat water plants by scraping them with filelike teeth.

53

SLUGS AND WORMS

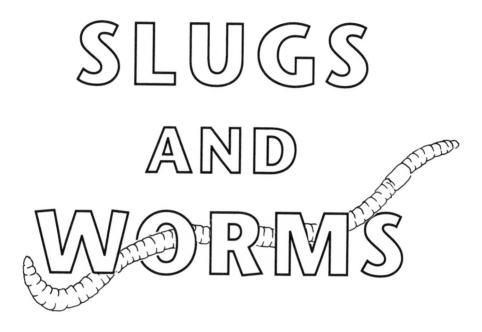

SLUGS

Field Gray Slug (*Deroceras agreste*)

Slugs, closely related to snails, have evolved over millions of years to survive without much of a shell. They have a small, thin piece of shell, called a mantle, under a fold of skin on their back. Having no shell makes it easy for them to squeeze into small places. To keep from drying out during the day, slugs hide under moist logs, rocks, and plants, or cover themselves with slime and burrow underground.

Slugs have long tongues covered with teeth, or radulae, which they use to scrape tender young plants. They use their small antennae for smelling and feeling. Their large antennae have eyes on the end. Both the small and large antennae can turn inside out and disappear into the body when touched. Slugs usually come out at night to feed— look for their slime trails in the morning.

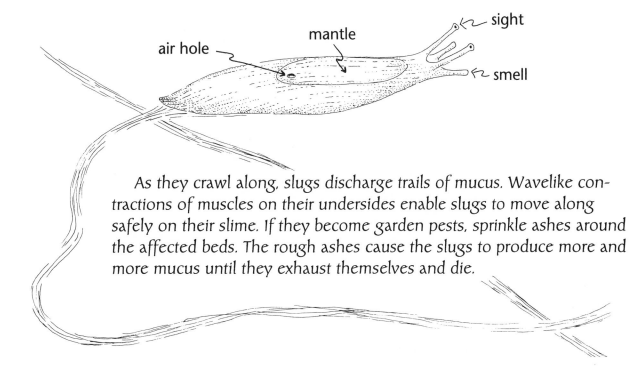

As they crawl along, slugs discharge trails of mucus. Wavelike contractions of muscles on their undersides enable slugs to move along safely on their slime. If they become garden pests, sprinkle ashes around the affected beds. The rough ashes cause the slugs to produce more and more mucus until they exhaust themselves and die.

Each individual contains both sexes, but it needs another slug for mating. In the soil, the slug lays hundreds of eggs, which hatch in about three weeks.

EARTHWORM

(Lumbricus terrestris)

Worms breathe through their skin, so they must stay moist. Earthworms can regenerate a new tail if too much isn't lost. They lack eyes but have light-sensitive skin at both ends. Worms also lack ears but can feel vibrations.

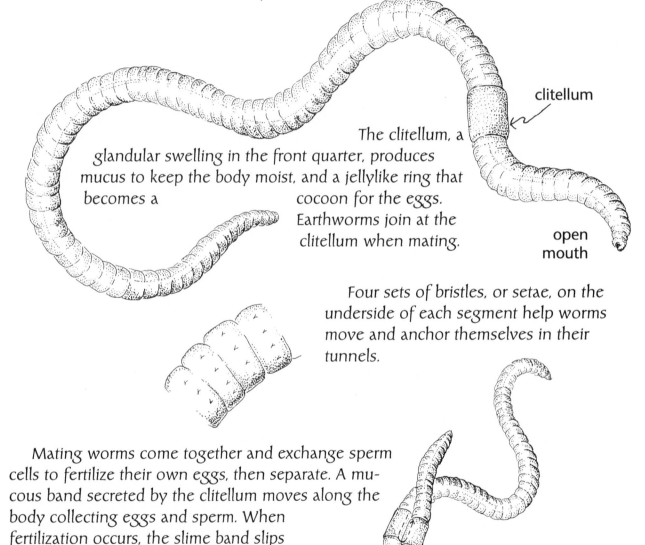

clitellum

The clitellum, a glandular swelling in the front quarter, produces mucus to keep the body moist, and a jellylike ring that becomes a cocoon for the eggs. Earthworms join at the clitellum when mating.

open mouth

Four sets of bristles, or setae, on the underside of each segment help worms move and anchor themselves in their tunnels.

Mating worms come together and exchange sperm cells to fertilize their own eggs, then separate. A mucous band secreted by the clitellum moves along the body collecting eggs and sperm. When fertilization occurs, the slime band slips off, the ends sealing to form a cocoon. Worms deposit the cocoons in the soil from May to July.

An earthworm has both male and female sex organs. The male sex organ is on the fifteenth segment. The female is on the fourteenth.

cocoon enlarged

A cocoon contains about 20 eggs, which hatch in one to five months.

Worms eat their way through the soil, digesting pieces of plants and other food. Excess soil, some organic matter, and mucus pass out the tail end, enriching the soil. Droppings left above ground in irregular humps are called castings.

Worms are extremely valuable soil dwellers. Their burrowing loosens the ground, turning it like a plow and letting in air and water. This process brings mineral-rich soil to the surface and buries plants and leaves, increasing the content of organic matter and thereby fertilizing the soil. Earthworm tunnels provide homes for small animals and insects.

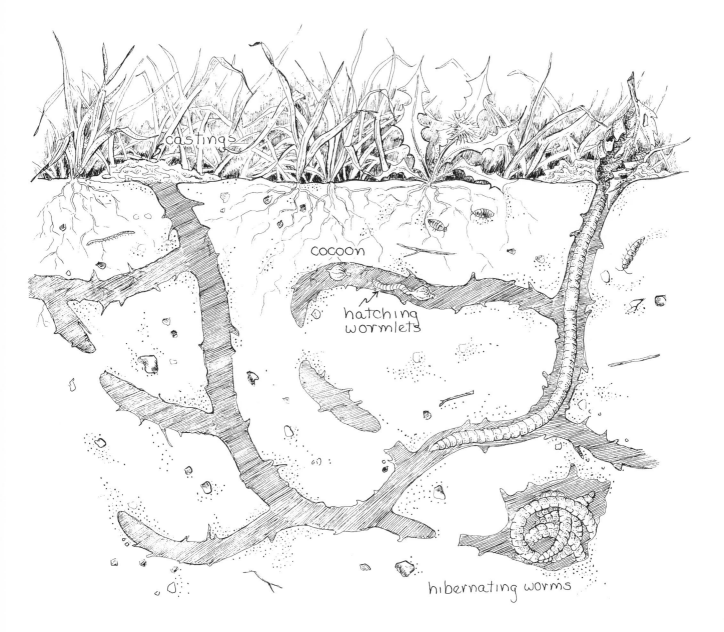

casting

cocoon

hatching wormlets

hibernating worms

INSECTS AND SPIDERS

ANTS
(family Formicidae)

The ant family has existed for 30 million years. Representatives of the more than 2,500 species are found all over the world except in the Arctic and Antarctic. All ants are social, meaning that different members have different jobs.

eggs
small, white

larvae
white, grublike, fed
liquid food by workers

pupae
white, some have silk
cocoons, other lack silk

2½ weeks

adults

Queen

The queen ant develops from a fertilized egg. After one mating flight, during which she is fertilized, the queen sheds her wings. She stores the sperm in her body to fertilize all her eggs. Once her colony is established, the queen's only task is laying eggs. Queens live a long time; some even reach 15 years of age.

Males

Males develop from unfertilized eggs; they have wings. Males do not work, not even feeding themselves. After mating with the queen in a spring swarming flight, the male ant dies.

Female Workers

Female workers develop from fertilized eggs; they are wingless. They spend their lives caring for eggs, larvae, and pupae, cleaning and enlarging the colony, and defending it against enemies.

Everyone knows about the strength of ants—they can carry loads many times their own weight.

To communicate, ants stroke antennae with one another then lick each other, exchanging drops of fluid. These drops contain chemicals from food and glandular secretions that tell other ants what kinds of food they've been near, where they have been, and with which other ants they have communicated.

Antennae allow ants to taste, smell, touch, and feel vibrations in the air. Without them, they are helpless.

After mating in the air with the males (who die soon after), the queen falls to the ground and tears off her wings. She digs a hole in the ground for a nest, enters it, and plugs it behind her. Her wing muscles turn to fat and nourish her. She lays her eggs and cares for her young, feeding them a salivary substance. Once raised, the first brood will care for the queen and enlarge the nest.

Nests vary. This is a typical one, showing the division of labor.

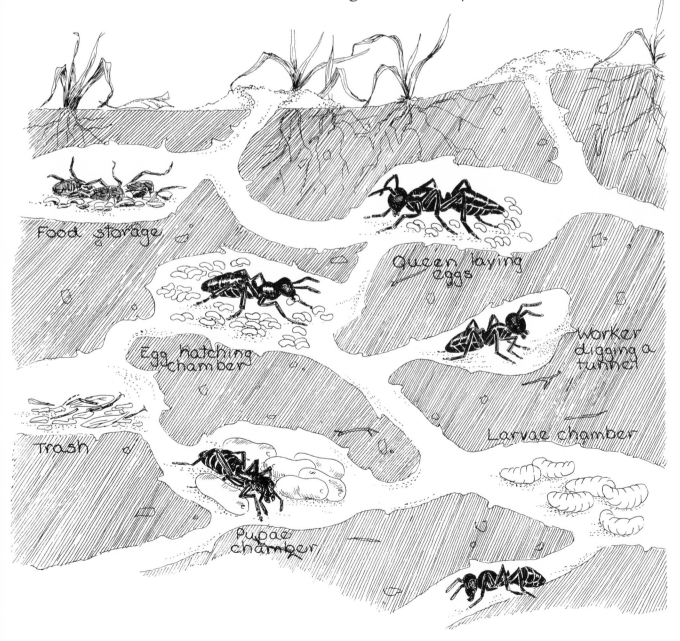

Food storage

Queen laying eggs

Egg hatching chamber

Worker digging a tunnel

Trash

Larvae chamber

Pupae chamber

BACK SWIMMER
(genus *Notonecta*)

underside

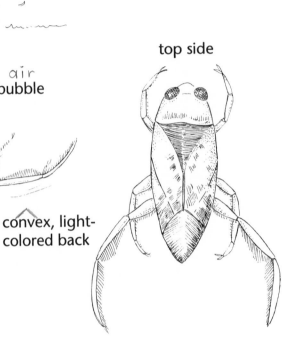

air bubble

top side

convex, light-colored back

This insect's name comes from its habit of <u>swimming underwater on its back.</u> The back swimmer uses its long, hairy, hind legs as oars. The legs also force air into an air chamber, a groove on its abdomen lined with hairs that holds air and enables the back swimmer to stay underwater for up to six hours. The <u>body is boat-shaped (con-vex)</u> with the <u>top a lighter gray-brown</u> than the bottom. The back swimmer spends much of its time resting at the surface, body and head angled downward. These aquatic bugs can bite, inflicting a <u>sting similar to that of a bee.</u>

flat back with dark, crossed lines

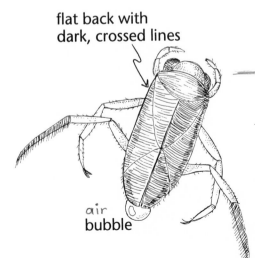

air bubble

Water Boatman
(genus *Corixa*)

The water boatman resembles the back swimmer but <u>swims right side up,</u> using its hind legs as oars and <u>moving more erratically</u> than the back swimmer. The water boatman's <u>top surface is flatter than the back swimmer's</u> and <u>has dark, crossed lines.</u> The water boatman uses its front legs to scrape up ooze and sweep it along with algae, dead leaves, and other sediment into its mouth. This insect <u>frequently clings to vegetation.</u> Every time it surfaces, the water boatman collects an air bubble under its outer wing covers.

BUMBLEBEE

(genus *Bombus*)

Bumblebees are large and fuzzy. They collect pollen on their hairy bodies and then comb it into baskets on their back legs. Bumblebees sting quickly if disturbed in their nest but are easygoing while looking for nectar. Unlike honeybees, who die after they sting, bumblebees can use their stingers again. If a bumblebee can't sting an enemy, it may squirt fluid from its abdomen tip as far as 15 inches in an attempt to repel the intruder. Like all bees, they are attracted to flower color. (Bees see ultraviolet and all the colors except red.) The bumblebee's long tongue enables it to collect nectar from deep flowers, such as red clover and snapdragons.

Bumblebees like to nest underground in abandoned holes and above ground in grass or hollow trees.

Fur insulates their large flying muscles so they do not need a "warm-up" period. That allows bumblebees to start feeding earlier in the morning than other bees can.

Bumblebees are social, but their colonies are smaller (only 100 to 400 individuals) than those of honeybees. Only young, mated queens live through the winter, hibernating in soil or in decaying vegetation. In spring, the solitary queen starts a new colony.

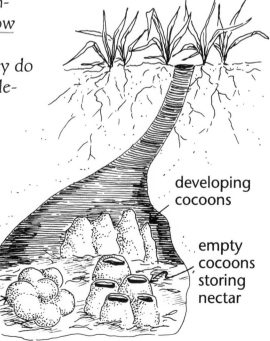

developing cocoons

empty cocoons storing nectar

eggs surrounded with balls of pollen

65

HONEYBEE

(Apis mellifera)

Although most bees are solitary, honeybees are social insects, with thousands living together and each doing its own job. There are three types of honeybees: workers, queens, and drones.

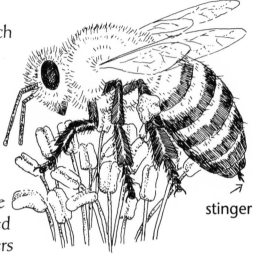

stinger

Workers' jobs are determined by age. In two months, they may have eight different jobs. They start out cleaning wax cells. Once nurse cells develop, workers feed larvae. After wax-producing glands form, workers build six-sided cells. Later, they cool the hive with their wings or watch over the queen. They concentrate nectar and can also be called on to guard the hive. After about three weeks, workers start to gather pollen and nectar. Because this is hard, risky work, the worker bee usually dies or is killed within seven or eight weeks of its birth.

A worker has a barbed stinger for self-defense but can use it only once. When the bee pulls away, the stinger and poison sac rip from its body and the bee dies. By reflex action, the stinger keeps moving deeper.

The queen has a long, tapering abdomen and spends her life laying eggs (up to 2,000 a day). She may live up to five years. To survive winter, she surrounds herself with workers for warmth. The queen uses her stinger only against other queens.

Drones (males) develop from infertile eggs. Their only job is to fertilize the queen. Only the strongest can fly high enough to mate, after which it dies. By fall, any remaining drones, no longer needed, are thrown out of the hive to starve. The drones have much larger eyes than workers do. A drone has no stinger.

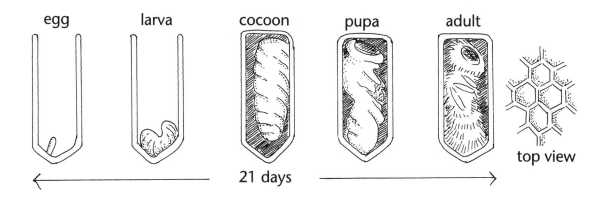

egg   larva   cocoon   pupa   adult

top view

← 21 days →

The six-sided wax cells adjoin others on all sides. That saves on material and gives added strength. The brood cells hold eggs and developing larvae. Workers feed larvae royal jelly (a mixture of honey, pollen, and fluid from the nurse glands) for the first 60 hours. Then some are fed just honey and pollen and become workers. Those left on the diet of royal jelly become queens. After 21 days, adults emerge from the cell.

Bees are the most important pollinators of crops. While gathering nectar, the bee's body becomes covered with pollen. Bristlelike hairs on the forelegs comb and pack pollen into baskets on the hind legs. Each bee visits many flowers of the same species, exchanging pollen between the flowers and thereby fertilizing them.

pollen

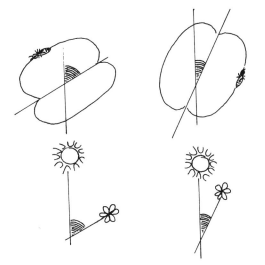

Honeybees dance to convey information on the location of food. The angle between the vertical and the center of the dance circle is the same as the angle between the food and the sun.

Bees form honey by blowing air into nectar to condense it. Three ounces of nectar produces one ounce of honey. All the nectar collected in a bee's lifetime may equal only four drops of honey. Adults eat nectar for energy and pollen for proteins and vitamins.

MONARCH BUTTERFLY

(Danaus plexippus)

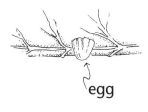

egg

Female monarch butterflies who have mated in their wintering grounds in Mexico head north toward Canada, laying eggs one at a time along the way. The adults from these eggs live only one month but produce another generation that lives long enough (ten months) to finish the migration north. The butterflies lay turban-shaped eggs on tender young milkweed and dogbane, which become food for the hatchlings. The young hatch in four days.

The larvae absorb poisons (cardiac glycosides, a heart stimulant) from feeding on the milkweed and accumulate them in their tissues. Animals that eat the larvae, pupae, or adults react to the poisons by vomiting. Through trial and error, predators learn not to eat monarch butterflies.

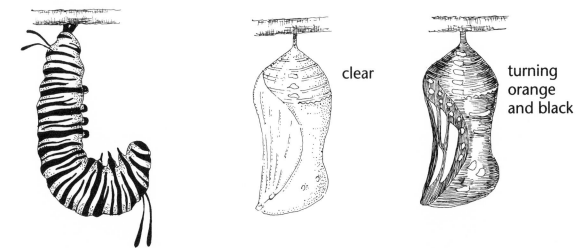

clear

turning orange and black

A clear chrysalis forms to protect the pupa while it undergoes metamorphosis. Through the clear capsule, you can see the monarch's color change from green to the black and orange of an adult. The monarch spends about twelve days in the chrysalis before emerging as an adult.

The adult emerges with its wings compressed and wet. It has to force fluids from its body into its wings to expand them. You can tell the male by the black spot (a scent gland) on the third vein of the hind wing.

Monarch butterflies are unique because they migrate seasonally. Some fly from Canada to Mexico, their primary wintering grounds. They have unusually large thoraxes and powerful muscles for long flight. Monarch butterflies assemble in large groups in the same places each year to prepare to migrate. You may see them covering trees like leaves as they ready themselves for their long flight. Approaching cold fronts or falling barometric pressure may spark their mass movement. When they arrive at their wintering grounds, the monarch butterflies rest in trees in a semitorpid state. In early spring, they head north individually. Many don't make it.

MOURNING CLOAK

(Nymphalis antiopa)

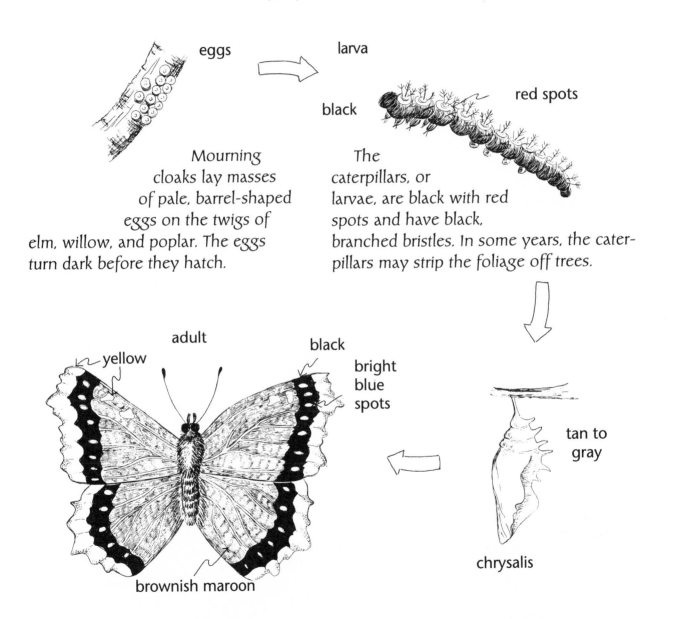

eggs

larva

black

red spots

Mourning cloaks lay masses of pale, barrel-shaped eggs on the twigs of elm, willow, and poplar. The eggs turn dark before they hatch.

The caterpillars, or larvae, are black with red spots and have black, branched bristles. In some years, the caterpillars may strip the foliage off trees.

adult

yellow

black

bright blue spots

tan to gray

chrysalis

brownish maroon

Mourning cloaks hibernate as adults, not as larvae, under bark, logs, or rocks. They are usually the earliest butterflies seen in spring, and you may even see them on warm winter days. The drab underside of their wings camouflages them perfectly against the bark. Mourning cloaks have a long life span of eight months, second in length in North America only to monarch butterflies.

CADDIS FLY

(order Trichoptera)

The larval stage of the caddis fly is aquatic. Each species lives in a specific watery habitat: lake shore, quiet stream, pond, swift current. Each also builds its own characteristic house: a tube of silk covered with sand, shells, sticks, pebbles, or plant pieces. Hooks on the back end of the larva hold it tightly to the case. The larvae typically drag their cases around underwater while they search for algae, leaves, twigs, and other vegetation or small aquatic insects to eat. These cases provide camouflage and act as ballast for the larvae, helping hold them on the bottom.

shells

sticks

sticks

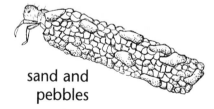

sand and
pebbles

sticks

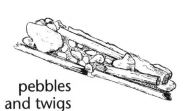

pebbles

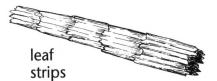

leaf
strips

sand

pebbles
and twigs

pebbles

Several species of caddis fly make
nets to gather food in flowing water.
They anchor the net to sand, rocks, or
logs, then hide at the side in a loose
shelter of silk and sand.

larva outside its case

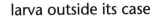

When the larva has finished growing, it attaches its case to the stream
bottom, seals the entrance, and pupates.
A few weeks later it leaves the case,
swims to the surface, splits its skin, and
emerges as an adult.

adult

FIELD CRICKET

(Gryllus assimilis)

female's ovipositor

Field crickets are common in woods, grass, gardens, and under rocks and logs. When the weather turns cold, crickets commonly come into houses.

You can tell the male and female apart by the female's long ovipositor. She uses it to lay eggs in holes in the ground in fall. These eggs hatch when the ground warms in spring.

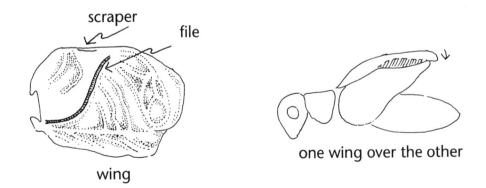

scraper

file

wing

one wing over the other

Crickets are known for their happy chirping, but actually only the male makes the sound. Each of its wings carries a filelike vein and a rough scraping ridge. The male raises its wings at a 45-degree angle and rubs the file of one wing against the scraper of the other. The vibrations produced result in the familiar chirp. Crickets chirp the loudest in warm weather. The males try to attract females or warn off other males with their calls.

DAMSELFLY

Civil Bluet (*Enallagma civile*)

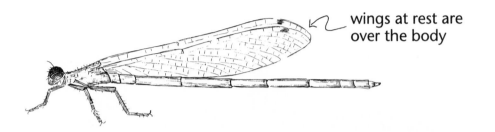

wings at rest are
over the body

This delicate insect resembles the dragonfly, but it has a more slender body and holds its wings above its back when at rest. The dragonfly holds its wings at right angles to its body when resting. The damselfly flies slowly, staying near cover and water.

The aquatic damselfly nymph eats anything it can catch. It has three platelike gills on its tail that enable it to breathe underwater.

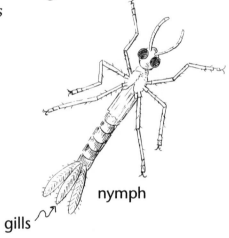

nymph

gills

male

female

The damselfly mates in a position similar to that of the dragonfly. Before mating, the male transfers sperm from the end of its abdomen to a storage chamber near its head. The male then holds the female by the neck, and she reaches her body around to accept the sperm. Their bodies end up contorted into a heart shape.

DRAGONFLY

Green Darner *(Anax junius)*

The dragonfly, one of the oldest insects, has existed for 300 million years. Of the 5,000 to 10,000 species of dragonflies, the green darner is one of the largest. You will usually find it near ponds and swamps. It is one of the few insects that migrates in winter.

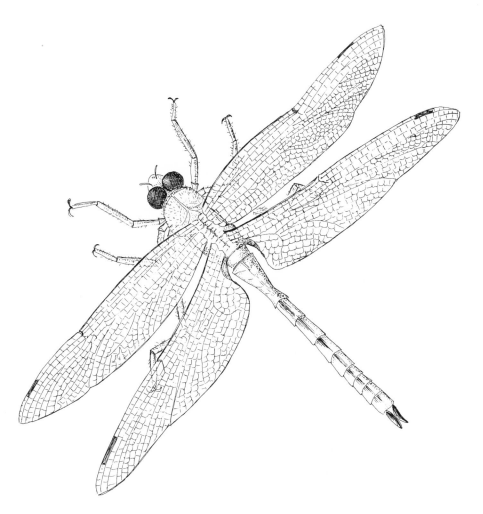

As it flies, the green darner holds its bristly legs together, forming a basket to scoop prey, such as bees, moths, horseflies, butterflies, and mosquitoes, from the air. It may also skim the surface of the water for food.

Although the dragonfly's wings are only 0.003 mm thick, they are powered by large thorax muscles that enable some dragonflies to fly up to 60 miles per hour. The pairs of front and back wings vibrate in opposition, stabilizing the insect in flight. That allows the insect to stop in midair, hover, then dart quickly away.

Dragonflies mate while tumbling in the air. Some females lay their eggs on the water surface, allowing the eggs to sink to the muddy bottom. Others slit plant stems and insert the eggs. Still others lay them underwater. After two to five weeks, the eggs hatch into ugly nymphs.

underwater nymph

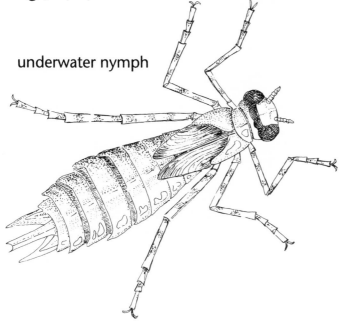

The voracious nymph will eat anything—tadpoles, small fish, insects. It breathes underwater with gills. When disturbed, the nymph forces water out its back end, which propels it quickly forward.

The nymph has a large lower lip (labium) with two claws on the end. When not in use, the labium folds up under the head. When the nymph spies prey, it whips out the labium, seizes the prey, and folds back the labium.

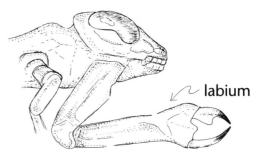

labium

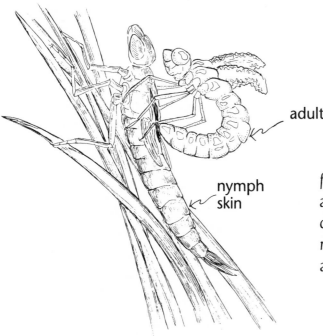

adult

nymph skin

A nymph usually sheds its skin, or molts, five or six times, though some molt as many as ten to fifteen times. A dragonfly spends one to five years as a nymph. During the last molt, the nymph climbs out of the water onto a stem, its skin splits, and the adult emerges.

FIREFLIES

(family Lampyridae)

In summer, fireflies start flashing at dusk and continue until about midnight. The flashing is a sex signal, usually emitted by the males in the air to females on the ground. The male's light glows twice as bright as the female's, and species differ in the rhythm of the flashes. The female of a certain species recognizes the male by the length of the flash. The male recognizes the right female by the time delay in her answering flash.

The larvae, many of which glow, live in the soil, greedily eating snails, worms, and other soft-bodied animals. After surrounding itself with mud, a larva changes to a pupa, which also may glow. An adult emerges ten days later. Adults consume no food.

A firefly is more than 92 percent efficient in transforming energy into light, while an ordinary light bulb is about 10 percent efficient. The firefly produces light when the organic substance luciferin and the enzyme luciferase react with oxygen.

Most fireflies contain a chemical substance that makes them unappetizing to birds and other predators.

larva

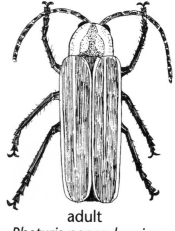

adult
Photuris pennsylvanica

77

WHITE-FACED HORNET

(Vespa maculata)

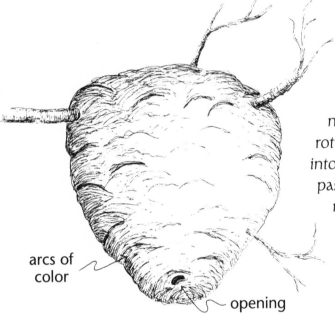

arcs of color

opening

White-faced hornets have black and white markings on the body and face. These hornets make large paper nests. To make this "paper," they collect rotten wood and plant stems and chew them into a paste moistened with saliva. When the paste dries, it turns papery. The outside of a nest may have bands of color from chips of painted wood the hornets have taken from houses and other buildings.

Inside the nest, many horizontal layers of cells open downward. For every layer of comb that is added, the hornets add a new coat of paper on the outside. The coat is added in arcs of quilted layers that trap air between them, providing maximum insulation.

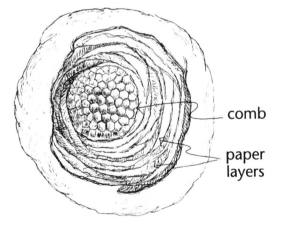

comb

paper layers

The queen lays eggs in the paper nest that hatch in one month. Workers develop first, then the male drones, and finally the new queens. Only the queen survives the winter, spending the cold season in dormancy in places like holes in old logs. The abandoned nest may be collected after a hard frost.

LACEWING

Golden-Eye Lacewing (*Chrysopa occulata*)

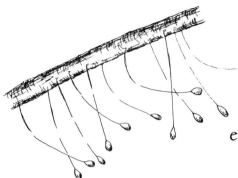

Lacewings place their eggs singly at the end of silk strands. The young are voracious eaters, but being on separate strands prevents them from eating each other when they hatch.

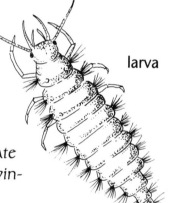

larva

After about five days, the eggs hatch. The larval stage lasts two weeks, during which time the young lacewings molt twice. The larvae feed greedily on aphids and other destructive insects. After spinning silky cocoons, the lacewings pupate for about 26 days—some overwinter in their cocoons.

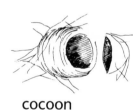

cocoon

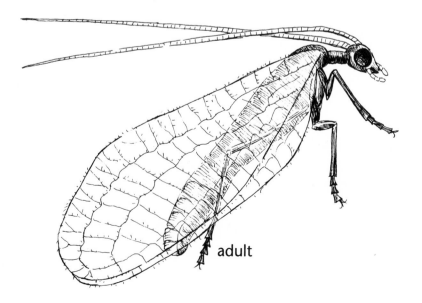

adult

The ⅘-inch-long adults are pale green, lacy, and delicate. They produce an offensive odor, probably for protection, that you can smell if you get close enough. The adults, like the larvae, eat many aphids.

LADYBUG

Two-Spotted Ladybug (*Adalia bipunctata*)

aphids

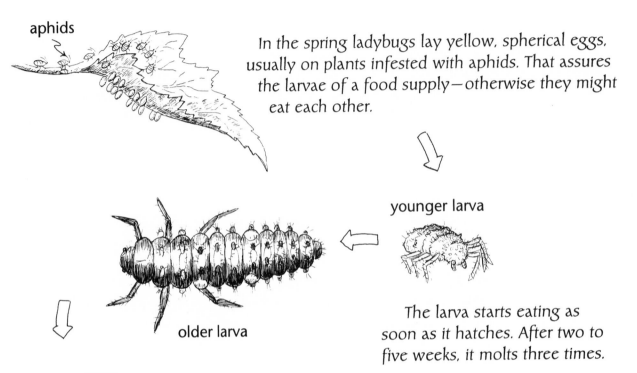

In the spring ladybugs lay yellow, spherical eggs, usually on plants infested with aphids. That assures the larvae of a food supply—otherwise they might eat each other.

younger larva

older larva

The larva starts eating as soon as it hatches. After two to five weeks, it molts three times.

The larva fastens its tail to a leaf, splits its skin, and pupates. After one week, an adult emerges.

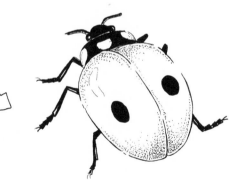

The ladybug's colored back is a modified front wing, which forms a shield over the back.

Ladybugs eat a large variety of harmful insects—one beetle can eat up to 60 aphids a day. Consuming stored fat, large groups of ladybugs hibernate together through the winter in hidden places. They can be collected commercially and won't be harmed if kept cold. Other common species resemble the two-spotted ladybug but differ in the number of spots (2, 9, 15, etc.).

PRAYING MANTIS

European Mantid (*Mantis religiosa*)

A better name for this insect would be "preying" mantis, in recognition of its ability to capture prey on the wing.

This ferocious eater feeds on ants, aphids, bees, flies, spiders, and other insects. If confined with other praying mantises, they may become cannibalistic. The praying mantis's spiny front legs, usually held as if in prayer, are designed for grasping. It is one of the few insects that can turn its head from side to side.

After mating, the female crawls upside down on a branch and oozes white foam from her back end. Inside the froth lie hundreds of eggs. The egg case turns brown and hardens quickly, protecting the eggs inside over the winter.

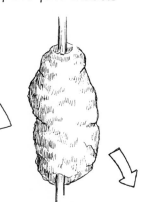

hardened
egg mass

Inside the egg case, narrow shafts ventilate the eggs. In spring, the case absorbs moisture and becomes soft and spongy. The young go down the shafts, attached to each other by silk cords, spill out, and are free. By the time they become adults, they will have molted up to nine times.

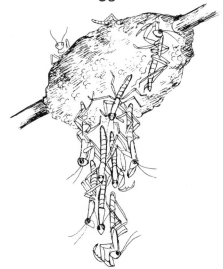

MOSQUITO

(genus *Culex*)

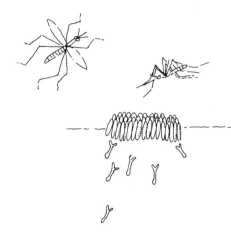

Mosquitoes lay their eggs, up to many hundreds, in rafts floating on water. After one or two days, the larvae (called "wrigglers" because they move by thrashing around) hatch. They stay near the surface and breathe through a tubelike siphon. Larvae eat tiny plants, animals, and inorganic debris constantly. They grow quickly and become pupae by the fourth molt.

Pupae (called "tumblers" because they are so active) stay close to the surface, breathing through a pair of tubes. After two to four days, they stretch out and swallow air until their skin splits. The adults step out, let their skin harden, then fly away.

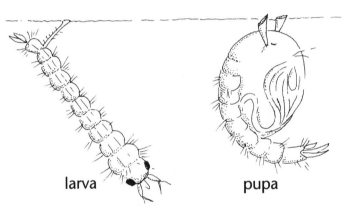

larva   pupa

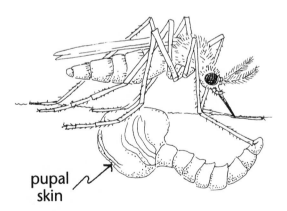

pupal skin

double tube surrounded by six piercing stylets

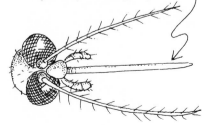

The male has more feathery antennae than the female, sucks only plant juices, and lives just a week. The female may live four to five months. She is attracted to animals by their exhaled breath. A double tube for piercing the skin and sucking blood forms her mouth. When she bites her prey, she injects saliva through one tube to prevent blood clotting. She sucks blood into her body through the other tube. The concentrated protein in blood ensures development of her eggs. The saliva causes the itch of mosquito bites. Through their saliva, certain species of mosquito transmit organisms that cause yellow fever, encephalitis, and malaria.

SPITTLE BUG

(Philaenus spumarius)

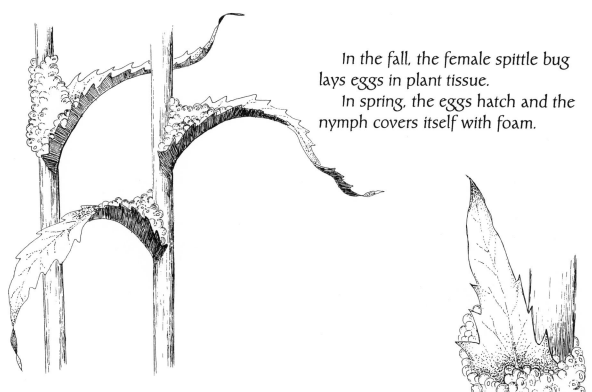

In the fall, the female spittle bug lays eggs in plant tissue.
In spring, the eggs hatch and the nymph covers itself with foam.

The nymph sucks the juice of the plant, which passes out the tail end as a liquid called honeydew. The bug blows air onto the liquid to make it foamy. The sticky foam holds its shape to provide shelter for the nymph— protecting it from the sun, keeping it moist and at a constant temperature, and hiding it from its enemies.

nymph (enlarged)

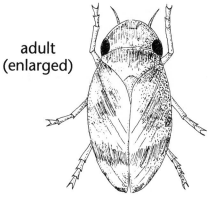

adult (enlarged)

When the spittle bug becomes an adult and grows wings, it leaps or flies from plant to plant.

MUD-DAUBER WASP

(genus *Sceliphron*)

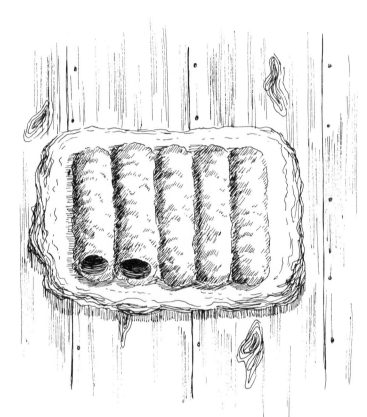

The female mud-dauber wasp builds several tubular cells of mud 1 inch long and ¼ inch wide under the eaves of houses and sheds. The wasp then places one egg plus several paralyzed spiders in each cell and seals it.

When the larvae hatch, they feed on the living, paralyzed flesh of the spiders. They overwinter as larvae, then pupate in spring.

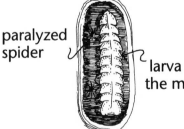

paralyzed spider

larva inside the mud cell

Mud-dauber wasps eat spiders that control plant-destroying insects.

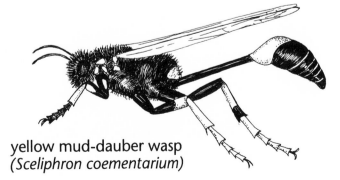

yellow mud-dauber wasp
(*Sceliphron coementarium*)

84

PAPER WASP

(genus *Polistes*)

Paper wasps make their nests of paper they create by chewing plant fibers and wood from trees and buildings. The wasps chew the pieces, add saliva, and form the cells of the nest from the paste. A single thread attaches each nest to the building. The tops of the cells, which open downward, are coated with a shiny, water-resistant substance licked on by the female. Look for the paper wasp's nests in protected places in old barns and other buildings.

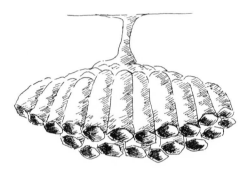

The female lays an egg in each cell. Larvae hang head downward, and the female feeds them insects and nectar. When the larvae are ready to pupate, the female seals each cell. The insect pupates inside, wrapped in a silk cocoon.

Paper wasps mate in the fall, after which the male dies. Only females survive the winter to build the nest in the spring. They also do all the caring for the young.

The paper wasp is long and slender, dark brown to black, with red spots and several yellow rings on the abdomen.

WOOLY CATERPILLAR

(Isia isabella)

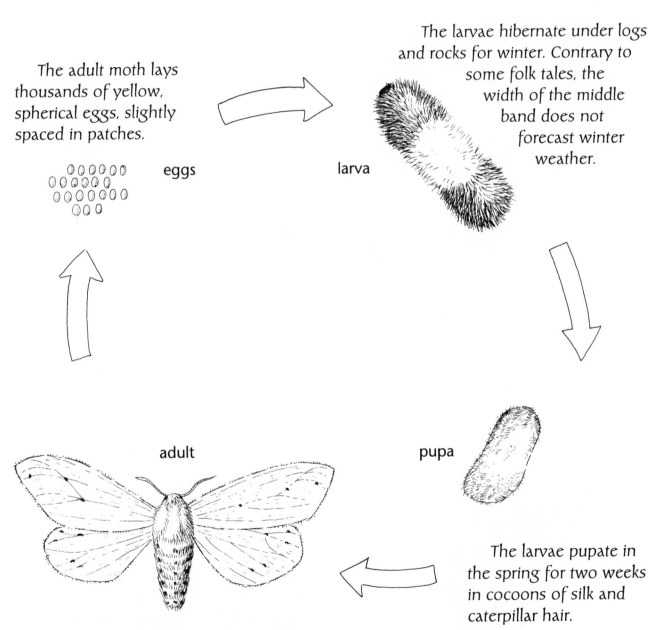

The adult moth lays thousands of yellow, spherical eggs, slightly spaced in patches.

eggs

The larvae hibernate under logs and rocks for winter. Contrary to some folk tales, the width of the middle band does not forecast winter weather.

larva

pupa

The larvae pupate in the spring for two weeks in cocoons of silk and caterpillar hair.

adult

Isabelle Tiger Moth *(Isia isabella)*
An adult emerges from the cocoon.

DADDY LONGLEGS

(Liobum vittatum)

Daddy longlegs, also called harvestman, is not a true spider (order Araneida). The daddy longlegs belongs to the order Phalangida and does not spin a web. It usually hunts at night for small insects, larvae, worms, spiders, fruit, and decaying or dead matter. Because the daddy longlegs's sight is poorly developed, it uses scent organs in its legs to locate prey.

Daddy longlegs has several strategies for escaping attacks. It can run very fast. Glands near the base of the front legs can squirt a foul-smelling liquid as far as 10 inches. Each leg has a weak spot where it can break off, then twitch for a while to distract the attacker. Daddy longlegs can live with the loss of several legs.

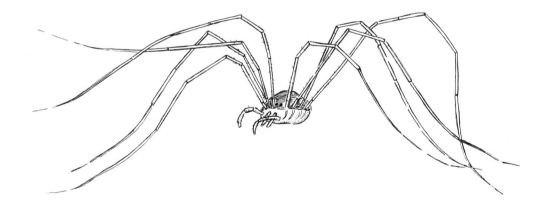

The daddy longlegs builds no web or nest. In the fall, the female lays twenty to thirty pale green eggs in leaf litter or soil. The eggs survive the winter and hatch in the spring. The adults gather in protected places such as woodpiles and overwinter in groups, but most don't survive.

GOLDEN GARDEN SPIDER

(Argiope aurantia)

The female golden garden spider's body is about 1 inch long; the male is smaller, about ¼ inch long. Both are covered with bright yellow or orange spots and bands. They use their fangs to poison their prey, then inject digestive juices into the prey, wrap them in silk, and suck out the resulting liquid later.

Glands in the spider's abdomen produce sticky and nonsticky liquid silk. Ducts carry the liquid silk to spinnerets, small projections at the back of the abdomen. There the spider weaves together hundreds of the fine threads. Once in the air the silk hardens, becoming stronger than steel for its weight.

spinnerets

silk

strengthening platform

sticky trapping spiral

The golden garden spider usually builds its roughly circular web at night. First it attaches a framework with irregular sides to supports. Then it lays down lines leading to the center like wheel spokes. In the center, the spider weaves a small spiral, attaching it to each spoke to strengthen the web. Finally it adds a larger outer spiral for trapping prey.

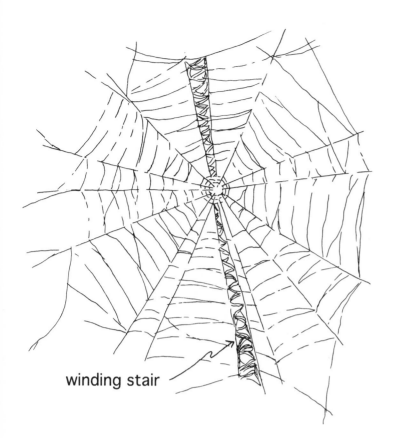

winding stair

The spiral is sticky for catching prey, the radii are not. Oil on the spiders' feet keep them from sticking to the silk. With the web finished, the spider weaves a ladderlike ribbon, called the winding stair, down the center. This may attract insects, strengthen the web, or just decorate the web. The male and female each spin similar but separate webs.

The female lays her eggs in the fall. First she spins dark brown silk over a mat of fluffy yellow silk. Next she lays about 100 golden eggs covered with sticky fluid.

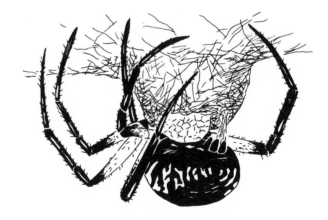

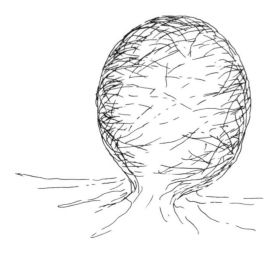

Finally she wraps her eggs in several layers of silk. The last layer turns dark and hard. Babies hatch during the winter but stay in their shelter until spring, when they chew their way free and float away on a line of silk.

SPIDER WEBS

All spiders produce silk but not all make webs. Sometimes spiders use the silk to wrap eggs, as draglines for moving from place to place, for ballooning (when the young use lines to catch the wind), or for wrapping prey. Spiders may have up to seven glands that produce seven different silks. Most spiders have at least five kinds. Spinnerets spin out the sticky fluid that solidifies into silk. Some strands stay sticky, others dry smooth. Oil on the spider's feet prevents it from sticking to the silk.

Funnel Web

The top of a funnel web is a wide sheet on which insects land. The spider hides in the funnel's hole and runs out to grab its prey. The only time it leaves the web is to build an egg sac.

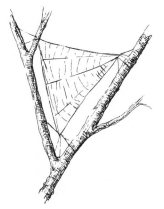

Triangle Web

A triangle web sits in the V between two intersecting branches. Insects are trapped when they land on or fly into the sticky strands.

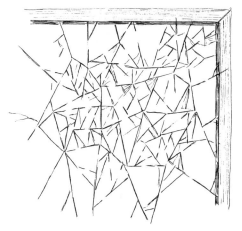

Cob Web

The cob web is an untidy tangle of loose strands attached by long threads to the corners and walls of windows, barns, and outbuildings. Prey are caught in the center.

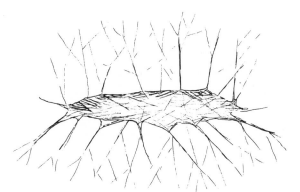

Sheet Web

A flat sheet of silk is formed with an irregular tangle above. When an insect hits the tangle of silk, it falls onto the sticky sheet.

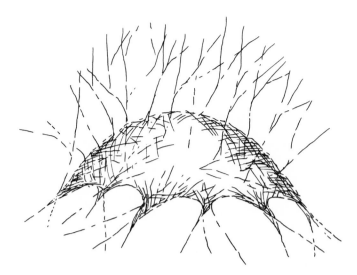

Dome Web

A dome-shaped web has an irregular tangle of silk above it. The spider hides under the dome, waiting for an insect to hit the tangle of silk and fall on the dome. Then the spider pulls its prey through the dome.

Orb Web

These beautiful webs are roughly circular. They rely on branches or walls to support them and so are never perfectly round. Some spiders remake their orb web each night; others just make repairs.

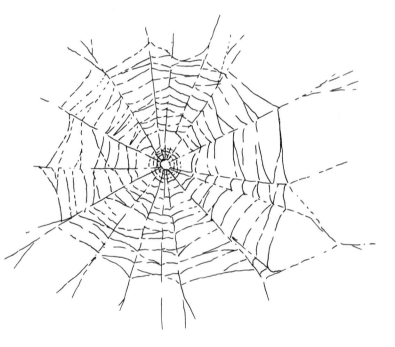

Ballooning

Young spiders spin silk lines to catch the wind and carry them through the air.

91

PLANTS

BERRIES

Some birds and other animals, such as bears, foxes, raccoons, and chipmunks, enjoy many of these berries—especially the juicy blackberries, raspberries, strawberries, and blueberries.

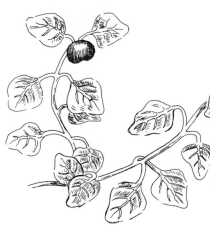

Partridge berry
(Mitchella repens)

The low, trailing partridge berry grows in woods and produces white-pink tubular flowers that bloom in pairs. A red, berrylike fruit with a dry, seedy taste forms from the coalescence of the two flowers. The shiny, green leaves and berries remain on the plant all winter.

Bunchberry
(Cornus canadensis)

This woodland plant has a whorl of leaves topped with a "flower" formed from four white, petal-like bracts. The bright red berries are pulpy and tasteless.

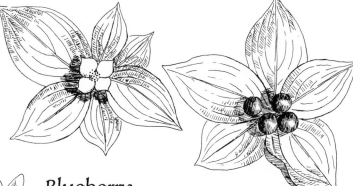

Blueberry
(Vaccinium angustifolium)

Blueberries thrive in the poor, acid soils of fields and roadsides. Small white flowers bloom in May or June. The delicious blue fruits ripen in July and August. In fall, the leaves turn a beautiful red.

Wintergreen
(Gaultheria procumbens)

This woodland plant keeps its leaves and berries all winter. The flowers of the wintergreen are small and bell shaped. The leaves and red berries smell and taste deliciously of wintergreen.

Blackberry
(Rubus allegheniensis)

Prickles cover the stout canes of the blackberry bush. The shiny black fruits, juicy with hard centers, make excellent pies, jams, and jellies.

Wild Raspberry
(Rubus strigosus)

Wild raspberries have prickly, erect canes and hollow, bowl-shaped berries. The luscious red fruits are high in vitamin C and, although smaller than cultivated raspberries, they have more flavor.

Serviceberry
(Amelanchier laevis)

This tree or shrub becomes covered with white blossoms before the leaves unfurl. Some people call this plant shadbush because it flowers when the shad run up the river. The red to purple fruit has a pleasant taste and several seeds.

Wild Strawberry

(Fragaria virginiana)

Wild strawberries grow at the edge of woods and in open fields. The white flowers have five petals. The fruit, though small, is sweet and delicious.

Elderberry

(Sambucus canadensis)

This shrub inhabits roadsides and moist areas. The tiny, white, fragrant flowers form in flat-topped clusters. Deep purple fruits develop in these clusters and are tasty in pies, wine, and jams.

Wild Cranberry

(Vaccinium macrocarpon)

Wild cranberry is a creeping, woody plant. The pink-white flower has four backward-pointing petals and anthers united into a pointed cone. The fruit, which is made into sauce and jelly, is dark red and tart. The plant commonly grows in bogs and swamps.

97

CATTAIL

(Typha latifolia)

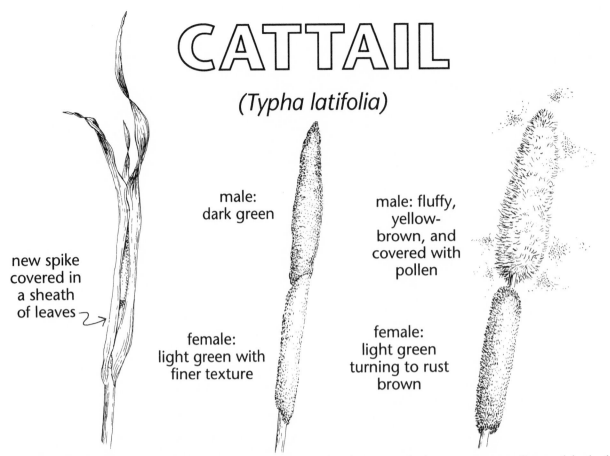

new spike covered in a sheath of leaves

male: dark green

female: light green with finer texture

male: fluffy, yellow-brown, and covered with pollen

female: light green turning to rust brown

Cattails grow in marshes, wet ditches, pond edges, and slow streams, favorable habitat for red-winged blackbirds, muskrats, and other wildlife. The flower spike consists of two parts. The male top part contains soft, fuzzy staminate flowers. The female bottom part has minute pistillate flowers.

After producing pollen, the male spike shrivels away. Once pollinated, the female spike develops into the familiar brown cattail, formed from tiny seedlike fruits. By the end of the summer the cattail disintegrates, releasing fluffy down attached to seeds. Birds and mice use the down in their nests.

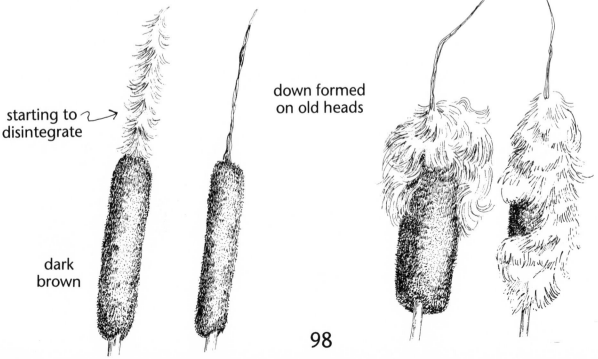

starting to disintegrate

down formed on old heads

dark brown

98

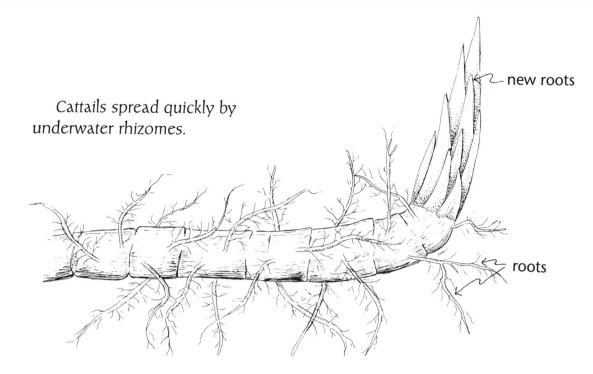

Cattails spread quickly by
underwater rhizomes.

new roots

roots

For Native Americans and early pioneers, the cattail was a source of food and useful materials. The rhizome can be dug all year, washed, peeled, dried, pulverized, and made into flour. In spring, tender new shoots can be eaten raw or simmered in salt water. The male spike, before it releases pollen, can be cooked and eaten like corn on the cob. Later the pollen can be collected and used as flour.

If gathered when green, dried, and then soaked, the long leaves can be made into rush chair seats. Dried stalks are good for starting campfires. At one time, the soft down was used to stuff mattresses and life rafts.

RED CLOVER

(Trifolium pratense)

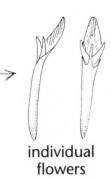

individual
flowers

Red clover is one of the best plants
for hay and honey production. The
flower head consists of a mass of florets
that resemble tiny sweet peas. The three
leaflets usually have a V marking.

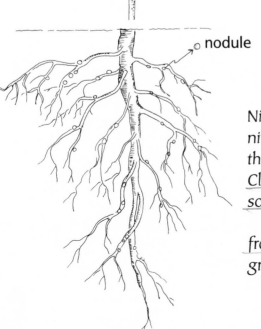

nodule

Clover is an important source of soil fertilizer.
Nitrogen-fixing bacteria in root nodules convert
nitrogen from the air into nitrogenous compounds
that can be used by the clover and other plants.
Clover is often planted in crop rotation to restore
soil fertility.

Red clover was introduced to North America
from Europe in the 1700s and now commonly
grows in old fields, along roadsides, and in lawns.

100

CONIFERS

Pine
(genus *Pinus*)
The pine has long and thin needles in bundles of five, three, or two.

Cedar
(genus *Cedrus*)
The cedar's needles are small, flat, and scalelike. They overlap along the twig.

Hemlock
(genus *Tsuga*)
The flat needles of the hemlock have two white lines (rows of stomata) on the underside. Short stalks attach the needles to the rough twig.

Balsam Fir
(*Abies balsamea*)
The flat needles of the balsam fir have two white lines on the underside and no stalk. The bare twig is smooth; needle scars lie flush with the surface of the branch. This fir is very aromatic.

Spruce
(genus *Picea*)
Recognize the spruce by its four-sided (square in cross section), pointed, stiff needles. Needles grow all around the twig, which is rough when the needles are gone.

Yew
(genus *Taxus*)
The yew's needles grow flat and stalked on a smooth bare twig.

Larch
(genus *Larix*)
This unusual conifer loses it needles in the fall. The soft needles grow in clusters on spurs and turn yellow before dropping off.

spurs

DANDELION

(Taraxacum officinale)

Each flower head of the dandelion contains many individual flowers, which look like yellow straps with toothed ends. The dandelion can bloom early because the blossoms unfurl in the center of the protective crown.

Some people make dandelion wine from the flower heads.

If gathered before flowers bloom, the rosette of leaves makes tasty salad greens or can be cooked and eaten like spinach. The greens are a good source of iron, potassium, calcium, and vitamins A and C.

The dandelion's deep tap root makes it difficult to eradicate this weed. Like a carrot, the root stores food for the plant. Some people cook and eat the root as a vegetable or, after slowly roasting it, grind the root into a coffee substitute.

The flower base arcs as it dries, positioning the light, downy seeds for dispersal by the wind.

enlarged seed

AMERICAN ELM

(Ulmus americana)

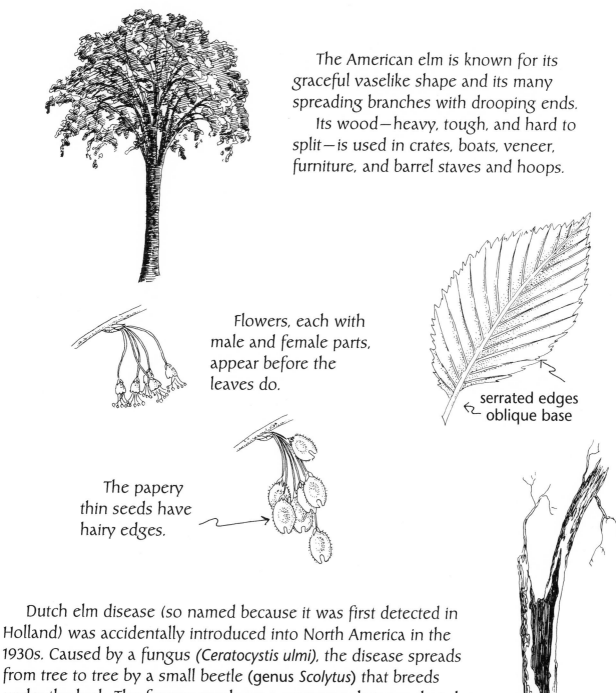

The American elm is known for its graceful vaselike shape and its many spreading branches with drooping ends.
Its wood—heavy, tough, and hard to split—is used in crates, boats, veneer, furniture, and barrel staves and hoops.

Flowers, each with male and female parts, appear before the leaves do.

serrated edges
oblique base

The papery thin seeds have hairy edges.

Dutch elm disease (so named because it was first detected in Holland) was accidentally introduced into North America in the 1930s. Caused by a fungus (*Ceratocystis ulmi*), the disease spreads from tree to tree by a small beetle (genus *Scolytus*) that breeds under the bark. The fungus produces a gummy substance that clogs the tree's water-conducting tubes. With the water supply cut off, the foliage wilts and the tree soon dies. No cure is known. To kill the beetles in the wood, remove infected trees and burn them immediately—don't store the wood for later use as firewood.

FERNS

(order Filicales)

One of the oldest plants, ferns appeared 350 million years ago. Their decomposing remains contributed to the formation of coal. Ferns grow in almost every habitat, even in the Arctic, but are most common in the tropics. They love damp, moist places.

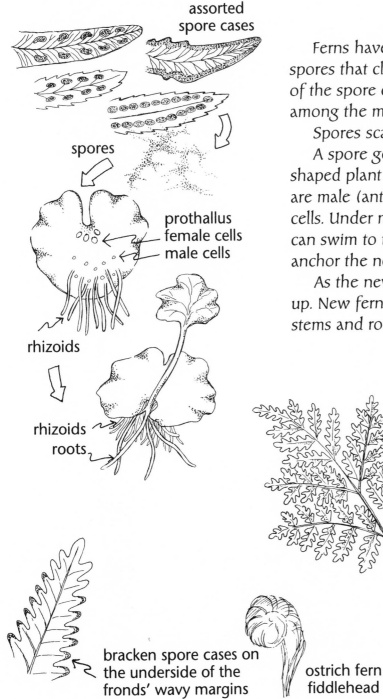

assorted spore cases

spores

prothallus
female cells
male cells

rhizoids

rhizoids
roots

bracken spore cases on the underside of the fronds' wavy margins

ostrich fern fiddlehead

Ferns have no flowers and reproduce with spores that cluster on the leaves. The distribution of the spore cases, or clusters of spores, varies among the many species of ferns.

Spores scatter only when dry.

A spore germinates into a tiny, flat, heart-shaped plant called a prothallus. On its underside are male (antheridia) and female (archegonia) cells. Under moist conditions (rain, dew), sperm can swim to the egg and fertilize it. The rhizoids anchor the new fern and take up water.

As the new fern develops, the prothallus dries up. New ferns also sprout from underground stems and rooting leaf tips.

Bracken Fern
(Pteridium aquilinum)

The bracken is one of the most common ferns.

If picked before un-coiling, the newly formed leaves, or fiddle-heads, of several varie-ties of bracken fern can be eaten as a vegetable. Simmer them in boiling water until tender or eat them raw.

BRACKET FUNGI

(class Basidiomycetes)

Bracket fungi grow like hard, leathery shelves on trees. Small pores on the underside point downward for protection from the rain. The fungi release their spores in dry weather. The mycelium—the thin, white network of filaments that grow like roots into the tree—absorbs food for the fungus. The filaments reach into the dead heartwood through wounds and can invade the living sapwood, weakening and even killing some trees as a result. Bracket fungi are found in a variety of colors and in many interesting shapes, sometimes resembling horses' hooves, turkey tails, umbrellas, or plates.

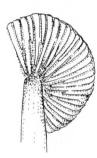

gills of a typical capped mushroom

pores of a bracket fungus

White Butt-rot
(Fomes applanatus)

White butt-rot grows on live or dead trees, usually oak, poplar, beech, maple, birch, or elm. This shelf fungus grows continuously year to year, forming ridgelike growth rings and often becoming quite large. White butt-rot is gray above and creamy white below.

GALLS

Galls are unusual and poorly understood growths on plants caused by flies, midges, aphids, mites, bacteria, and fungi. An insect enters the plant tissue to feed and lay eggs. The developing eggs secrete substances that cause abnormal but controlled growth in the plant. The resulting new structure provides a home and food supply for the insect larvae. Later, other creatures may make homes of the galls.

cut open

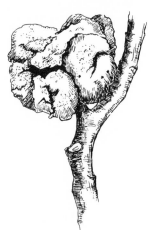

The oak apple gall is formed by a wasp larva on oak twigs and leaves.

The maple leaf spot gall is caused by mites on the maple leaf.

The gouty oak gall deforms oak twigs that contain many wasp larvae.

The spruce pineapple gall forms where an aphid lays eggs at the base of spruce needle buds.

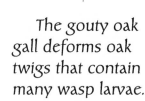

To form a willow pine gall, a gnat or midge lays eggs on the new growth at the tip of a willow branch.

In the blueberry stem gall, wasp larvae deform blueberry twigs.

  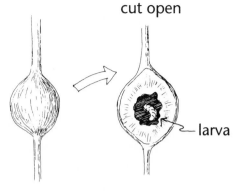

The goldenrod bunch gall results where a midge nests in the goldenrod's leaf bud.

The goldenrod elliptical gall is caused by a moth larva in the bud end of a goldenrod.

The goldenrod ball gall forms where the larva of a fly burrows into the goldenrod's stem.

The pincushion gall on rose bushes is caused by wasp larvae.

The purse gall is caused by aphids invading poplar leaf stalks.

larva

cut open

In the willow petaled gall, a midge causes the willow's petals to modify.

The cherry black knot gall forms where a fungus enters cherry branches.

107

GOLDENROD

Canada Goldenrod (*Solidago canadensis*)

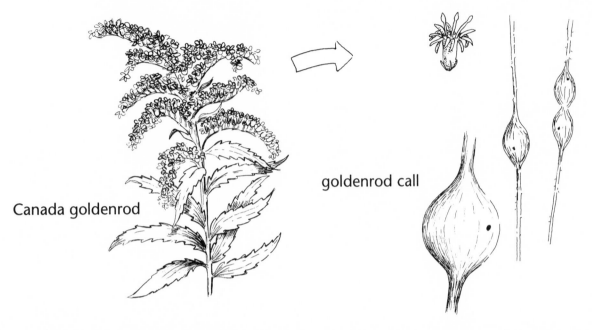

Canada goldenrod

goldenrod call

Goldenrod blooms from late summer to early fall, after many other plants have finished blooming. The bright yellow flowers attract a variety of insects, such as beetles, bees, flies, wasps, aphids, moths, butterflies, and spiders.

Galls commonly form on goldenrod stems. The gallfly lays its egg in the stem. When the larva hatches, it secretes a substance that causes the tissue to swell. In the spring, the larva chews its way out and soon becomes an adult.

Though some people may be allergic to goldenrod pollen, it may not cause as many allergies as its reputation suggests. The pollen is heavy and sticky and not likely to be carried on the wind. Ragweed pollen may be a worse culprit.

Some people use the young goldenrod leaves in salads and the dried leaves and flowers in tea. The seeds are a favorite winter food of many birds.

Goldenrod Shapes

slender   flat-topped   elm-branched   clublike   plumelike

108

HORSETAIL

(Equisetum arvense)

Horsetails thrive in poor soil, where they help anchor the soil. The ancestors of the horsetail lived in the Carboniferous Period (300 million years ago) and were the size of trees. The name comes from the resemblance of the whorls of branches to a stylized version of a horse's tail. The hollow stems contain large amounts of silica, which gives them a rough texture.

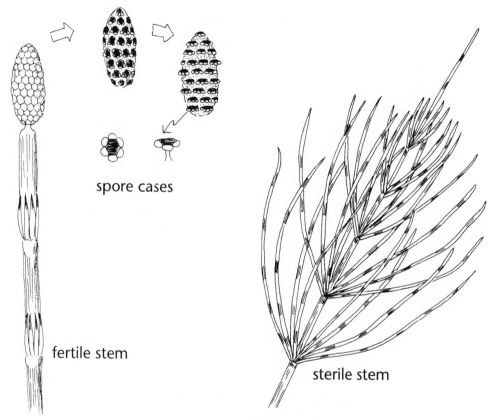

spore cases

fertile stem

sterile stem

Horsetails have two types of stems. Fertile ones grow from horizontal, underground sections. They are brown or flesh colored and end in a spike covered with spore cases. After the spores disperse and the stems wither, the sterile stems appear. These are green with whorls of branches.

Each spore case looks like an over-turned box out of which spores fall.

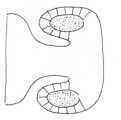

Four straps on each spore help scatter them. When dry, the straps coil up. When moist, they uncoil and catch the wind.

109

JACK-IN-THE-PULPIT

(*Arisaema triphyllum*)

spathe or "pulpit"

spadix or "Jack"

flowers

"Jack"

Jack-in-the-pulpit grows in moist, rich woods and thickets. The spadix, or "Jack," bears tiny male flowers and female flowers at its base. Sometimes the plant has only male or female flowers. A curving hood, called the spathe or "pulpit," envelops the spadix.

Beetles and small flies pollinate the flowers. Green berries, which turn scarlet, develop in the fall.

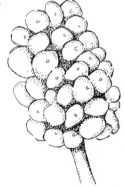

The plant rises from a turnip-shaped underground bulb. Native Americans ate the bulb. Because it contains calcium oxalate crystals, the bulb gives a burning feeling when eaten unless properly cooked.

110

JEWELWEED

(Impatiens capensis)

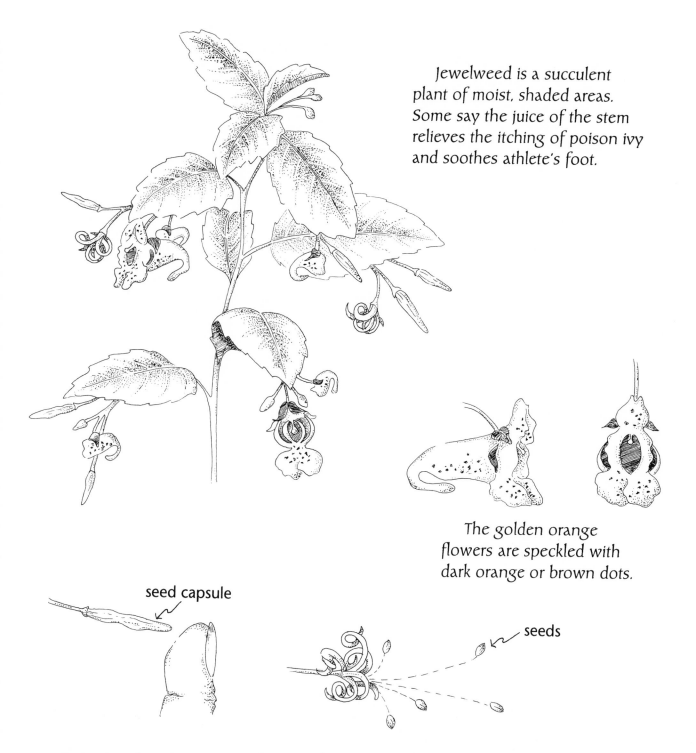

Jewelweed is a succulent
plant of moist, shaded areas.
Some say the juice of the stem
relieves the itching of poison ivy
and soothes athlete's foot.

The golden orange
flowers are speckled with
dark orange or brown dots.

seed capsule

seeds

Sometime between June and September, the slender seed capsule bursts, especially
when touched, and shoots the nut-flavored seeds several feet.

111

LICHENS

Lichens are fascinating organisms that inhabit some harsh places: under snow, in dry deserts, at high altitudes, and on hot rocks. They can survive at temperatures from -450 degrees F (-268 degrees C) to 424 degrees F, 212 degrees above the boiling point of water. Lichens subsist on wind-borne water and debris. Because lichens cannot grow in polluted air, biologists monitor their growth as indicator species of environmental health.

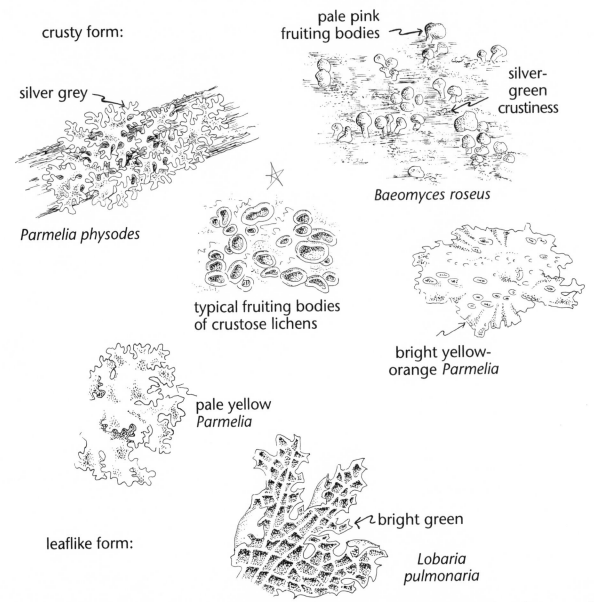

crusty form:

silver grey

Parmelia physodes

pale pink fruiting bodies

silver-green crustiness

Baeomyces roseus

typical fruiting bodies of crustose lichens

bright yellow-orange *Parmelia*

pale yellow *Parmelia*

leaflike form:

bright green

Lobaria pulmonaria

Lichens consist of two plants living together: an alga and a fungus. The alga provides food for both. The fungus provides protection from wind and sun, catches moisture, and furnishes the structure on which the alga is imbedded. Such a partnership of two organisms is called symbiosis. The lichen's name derives from the fungus.

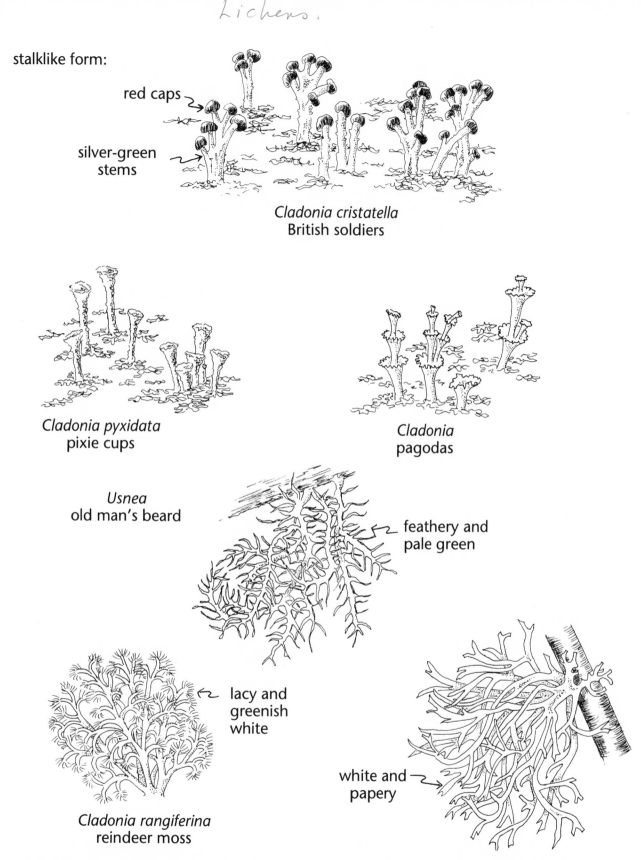

stalklike form:

red caps

silver-green
stems

Cladonia cristatella
British soldiers

Cladonia pyxidata
pixie cups

Cladonia
pagodas

Usnea
old man's beard

feathery and
pale green

lacy and
greenish
white

white and
papery

Cladonia rangiferina
reindeer moss

Lichens play an important role in the first stage in plant succession because they can grow in the poorest soil or even in rocks. Their acidic secretions and very slight expansions and contractions from growth and dryness cause the rock's surface to crumble. Over a period of time, this action forms soil for higher plants.

LEAF COLOR

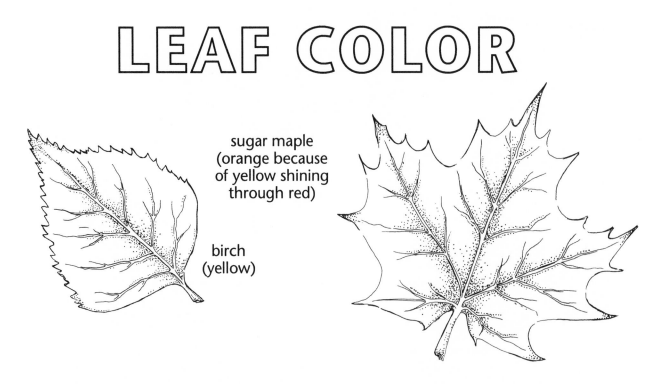

sugar maple
(orange because
of yellow shining
through red)

birch
(yellow)

Leaves are green because of the green pigment chlorophyll. In spring, when plants first begin to produce chlorophyll, leaves are light green. In summer, with more of the pigment present, leaves become darker.

The leaf cells also contain other pigments that chlorophyll masks in spring and summer. Xanthophyll is yellow, and carotene is yellow-orange. In fall, cells at the base of the leaf stalk, called the abscission layer, dry out. Water flow stops and chlorophyll production ceases, allowing the other colors to show through.

Red anthocyanin pigments are dissolved in liquids in plant cells. Plants with permanently red foliage contain the red pigments year-round. Other plants, such as oaks and maples, produce anthocyanins in the fall when sugar accumulates in the leaves. If warm nights follow warm days, anthocyanins and sugar go to the roots for storage. If nights are cool, sugar and anthocyanins stay in the leaves, creating spectacular fall colors.

Some trees, such as oaks, contain the chemical tannin, which when mixed with yellow and orange pigments turns leaves brown.

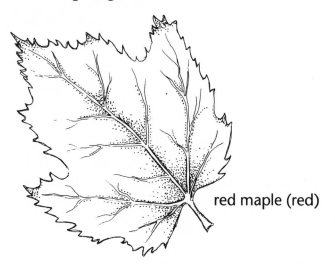

red maple (red)

oak (brown)

RED MAPLE

(Acer rubrum)

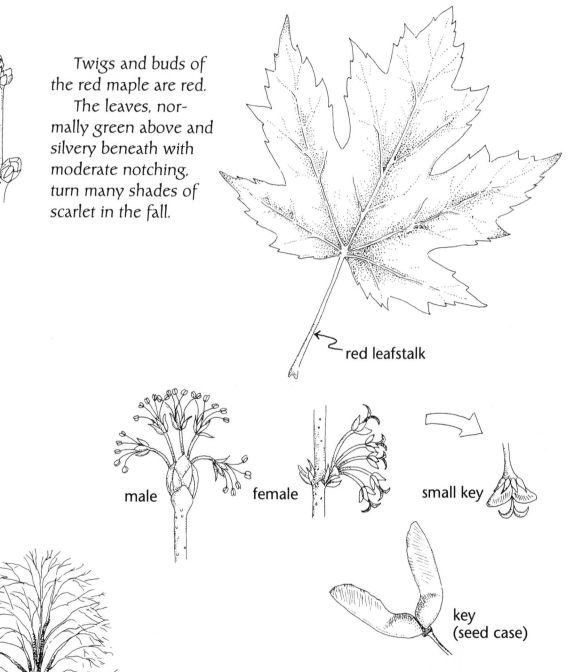

Twigs and buds of the red maple are red. The leaves, normally green above and silvery beneath with moderate notching, turn many shades of scarlet in the fall.

red leafstalk

male

female

small key

key
(seed case)

The crown is broad and oval above a short trunk.
The intense red of this tree's fall foliage helps make the New England and Maritime autumns among the most beautiful anywhere. Pioneers made ink and brown and black dyes from the bark of the red maple.

SUGAR MAPLE

(Acer saccharum)

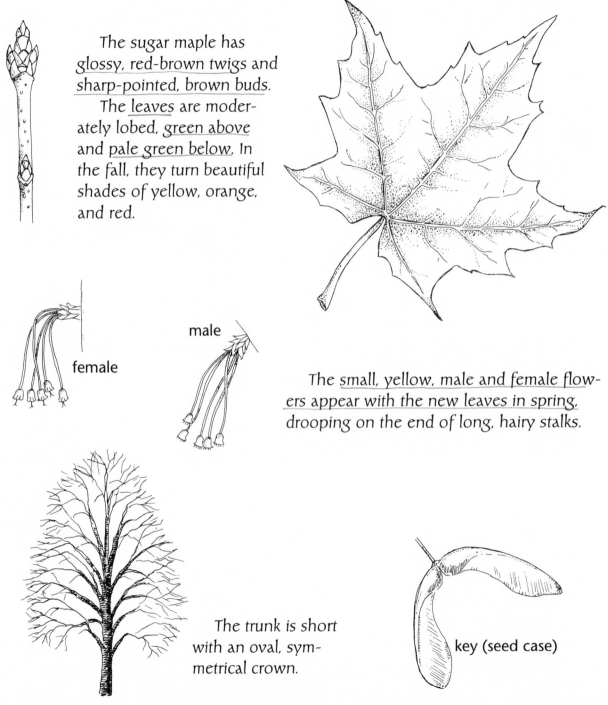

The sugar maple has glossy, red-brown twigs and sharp-pointed, brown buds.

The leaves are moderately lobed, green above and pale green below. In the fall, they turn beautiful shades of yellow, orange, and red.

female

male

The small, yellow, male and female flowers appear with the new leaves in spring, drooping on the end of long, hairy stalks.

The trunk is short with an oval, symmetrical crown.

key (seed case)

The wood of the sugar maple makes beautiful furniture and flooring and long-burning firewood. In spring, sugar maples produce abundant sweet sap that people collect and boil down into maple syrup.

MAPLE SYRUP

Sugar made by leaves during photo-synthesis remains stored as starch in the tree's roots, trunk, and branches through the winter. In spring, starch, which is not water soluble, slowly changes back to sugar, which can dissolve in sap. The sugar content of sap peaks in late winter to early spring, when nights are cold (averaging 23 degrees F) and days are warm (averaging 55 degrees F).

Covered buckets hang at the tap holes on the tree trunks. Modern operations may use plastic tubing instead of buckets to collect sap.

Although all maples have a sweet sap, the sap of the sugar maple is the sweetest.

Tapping does not injure the tree—the sugar taken is less than 10 percent of the tree's annual production.

About 40 gallons of sap make 1 gallon of syrup, depending on the sugar content. That will make about 8 pounds of sugar.

In the sugar shack, the sap is boiled down to evaporate the water and form syrup.

Acid rain seems to be killing sugar maples and decreasing the amount of sap collected.

MILKWEED

Common Milkweed (Asclepias syriaca)

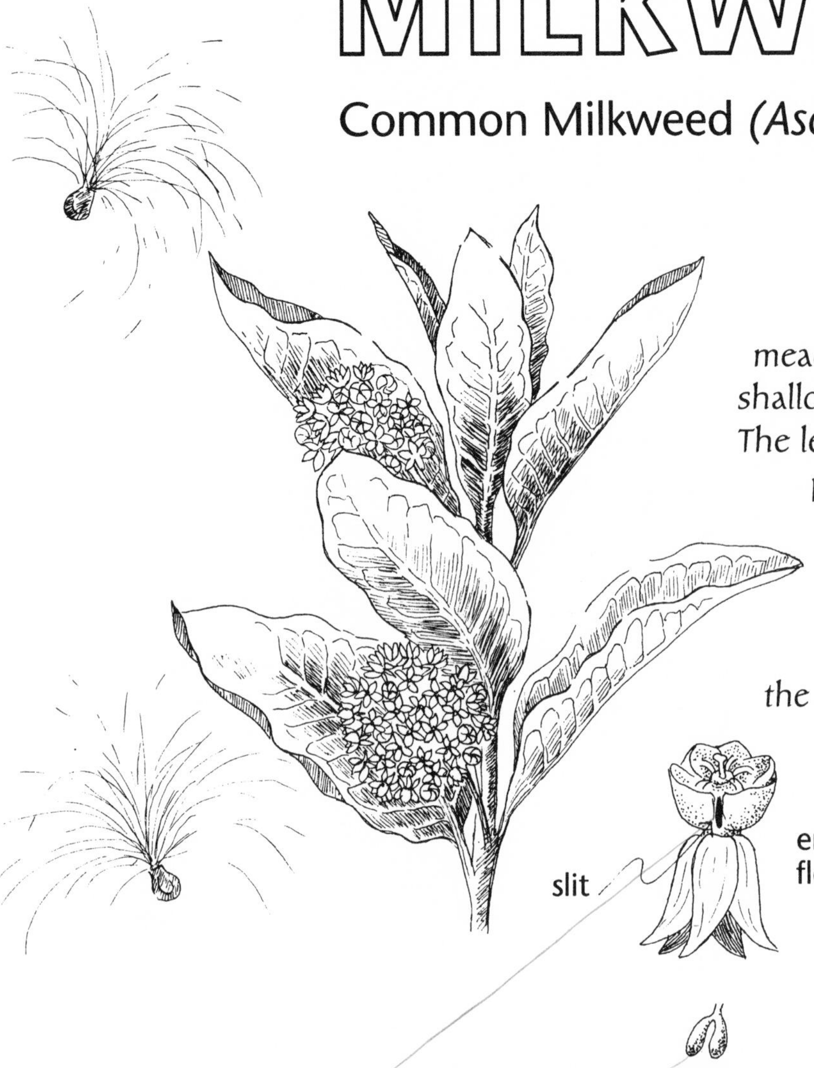

roadsides

Milkweed grows in open fields, meadows, and waste lots. The plant's shallow roots help prevent soil erosion. The leaves are thick and downy. The purple to pink flowers appear in round clusters. The milky sap contains cardiac glycosides. When monarch butterfly adults and larvae absorb these chemicals, the insects become toxic to predators.

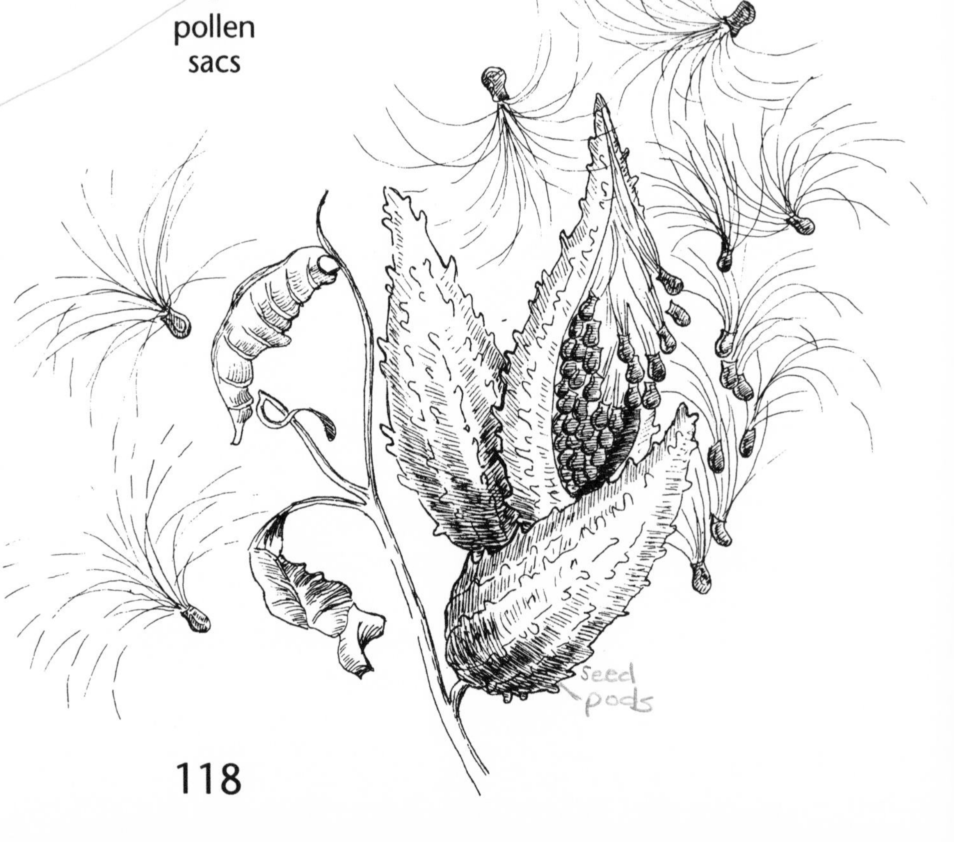

slit

enlarged flower

pollen sacs

tufted seeds

The feet of insects often slip into the slits in the flowers. When pulled free, they pull with them a pair of pollen sacs that the insect can carry to the next flower.

Soft projections cover the seed pods. The pods split open in the fall to expose the tufted seeds, which are released a few at a time. The wind carries them off, and if the fluffy hairs catch on something, the seed detaches and falls to the ground.

seed pods

118

MOSS

(class Musci)

Mosses reside in damp, shady places—from the Arctic, through the tropics, to Antarctica—growing in soft, dense mats on the ground, on rocks, and in trees. Mosses hold soil and water and prevent soil erosion. When moss dies, the vegetable matter it leaves behind helps to create new soil. Look for moss on all sides of trees, not just the north, but whichever area is the most shady and moist.

Life Cycle

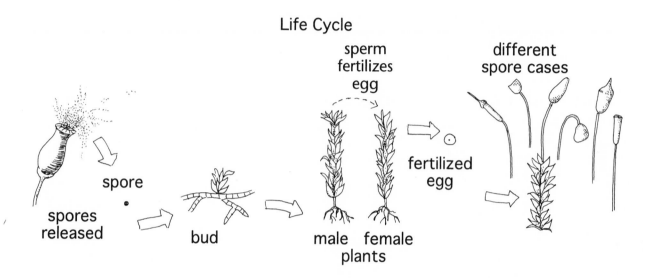

Spores pour out of capsules of a parent plant. A spore germinates and forms green threads, the first stage in development of the new organism. Buds on the threads form new plants—usually male or female. When conditions are moist, such as on dewy mornings, sperm cells from the male plant swim to the female and fertilize an egg cell. The fertilized egg grows into a capsule on a long stalk that stays attached to the parent. Different mosses have capsules of different shapes

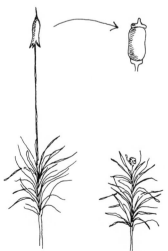

Hair-Cap Moss
(Polytrichum commune)

This moss grows in infertile places as well as in woods and on bog edges. Look for the typical closed-umbrella–shaped capsule of the hair-cap moss growing in shady areas of your lawn.

OAKS

(genus *Quercus*)

There are over 300 kinds of oaks in the world. Woodworkers prize their hard, heavy, and strong wood. Oaks grow slowly and enjoy long, fairly disease-free and insect-resistant lives. The bark of some oaks contains tannins, which are used for curing leather.

Oak twigs and acorns provide a large portion of the food supply of many birds and mammals, including rodents, squirrels, bears, deer, crows, jays, turkeys, grouse, and wood ducks. The success of many wildlife populations follows the cycle of the acorn crop. When the crop is small, some species of squirrel migrate, deer have fewer young, and bears produce fewer cubs. The number of predators decreases with the availability of prey.

The white oaks have strong, durable wood and leaves with smooth, rounded margins. The inner surface of their acorn cups are smooth, and the sweet, edible acorns mature in one year. In the red oak group, the leaves have bristle-tipped lobes, the inner surface of the acorn cup is woolly, and the bitter-tasting acorns take two years to mature.

Red Oak
(*Quercus rubra*)
The cup encases ⅓ of the nut. Scales on the cup are blunt and tightly overlapping.

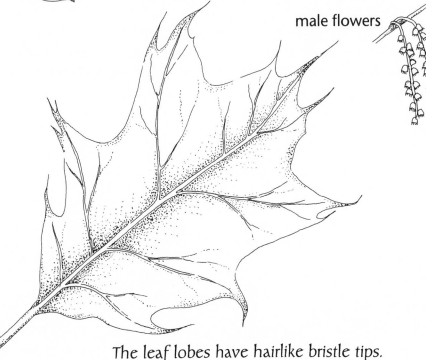

male flowers

female flowers

The large tree has a rounded crown and stout branches.

The leaf lobes have hairlike bristle tips. In the fall, the leaves turn brown or red.

POISON IVY
(Rhus radicans)

Poison ivy varies widely in form. It can grow as a vine, a shrub, or a single-stemmed plant. The yellow-white flowers bloom in clusters and mature as white berries that are an important winter food for wildlife.

The poison, present in all parts of the plant, is uroshiol, a yellow, volatile oil. On contact, it causes inflammation, blisters, extreme itching, and sometimes fever and swelling. The poison can also spread in smoke if the plants are burned. Washing with soap or alcohol immediately after contact should help lessen the rash. *How to treat.*

The leaves always grow in threes, but their edges can be smooth or notched in many combinations. They may be shiny or dull and turn bright red in the fall.

PUFFBALLS

Gemmed Puffball *(Lycoperdon gemmatum)*

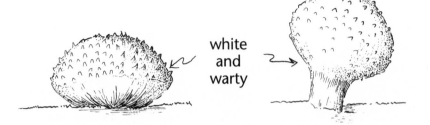

white and warty

Puffballs pop up in late summer and early fall, especially after rain. Most species of puffball are edible when the inside flesh is white and firm, though some people suffer allergic reactions to them. Once they lose their white color they cannot be eaten safely. Positive identification of any mushroom before you consider eating it is essential. This species grows near rotten wood, anchored in the soil by underground mycelial strands.

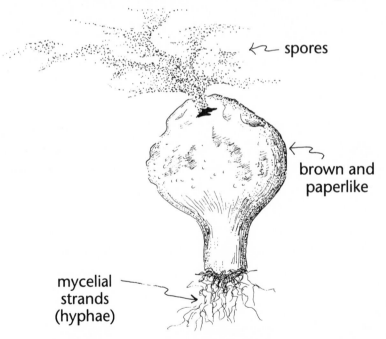

spores

brown and paperlike

mycelial strands (hyphae)

The mycelia, with the help of bacteria and other microbes, help in the decomposition of dead matter.

As the puffball matures, it shrivels and the outside turns brown and papery. At maturity, the thin skin holds a dry, powdery mass of spores. A small hole opens in the top of the puffball. The spores are so light that the slightest breath of air carries them out of the hole and away. A very small proportion of these spores develop into puffballs.

QUEEN ANNE'S LACE

(Daucus carota)

The flower heads of Queen Anne's lace are popular gathering places for wasps, flies, beetles, butterflies, bees, and spiders. The odor of the flowers may attract them.

This plant, closely related to our domestic carrot, commonly grows in fields and pastures. As a biennial, it produces only a rosette of leaves and an underground, carrotlike taproot in the first year. In the second year, it produces a flower stalk.

The bristly seeds, each with four rows of spines, catch easily in animal fur and get carried to other places. The seeds, which persist in the soil a long time, can be used whole to spice soups and salads or steeped as a tea.

The intricate flower heads look lacy. In the center of the flower head is usually one red-brown flower that may attract insects that mistake it for another insect. The flowers open when the humidity is high and close when the humidity is low.

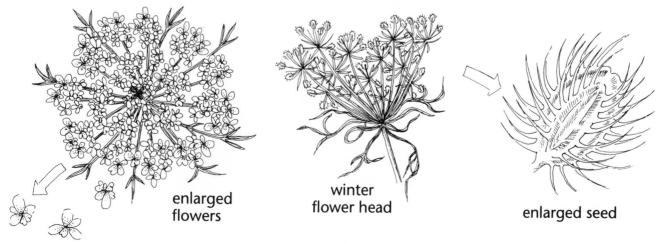

enlarged
flowers

winter
flower head

enlarged seed

WILD ROSE

Virginia Rose (*Rosa virginiana*)

More than 20 species of wild rose live in woods, uplands, and wetlands of this region. The flowers, pink and fragrant, have yellow stamens and pistils in the center. The thorny shrubs provide good cover for birds and mammals.

hip

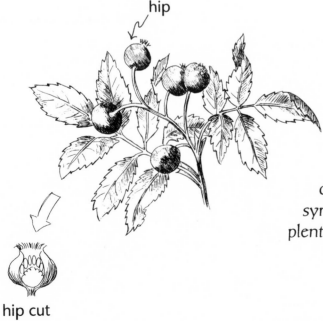

hip cut
open

The reddish fruits, called rose hips, remain on the plant all winter and are a valuable food for birds, deer, opossums, coyotes, and bears. The hips are very rich in vitamin C—three small hips contain as much vitamin C as one large orange. Hips are easily collected and dried for use in jams, tea, syrup, or as a snack—but be sure to leave plenty for the wildlife.

SKUNK CABBAGE

(*Symplocarpus foetidus*)

Skunk cabbage grows in swamps and marshes and will even emerge while snow is still on the ground. The cells divide rapidly, producing heat that can thaw nearby snow.

spadix

A mottled hood appears around a fleshy, spongy spike, or spadix. Small flowers cover the spike. A strong, offensive, skunky odor attracts flies and gnats—not bees or butterflies—to do the pollinating. Both the color and scent of the flowers mimic those of dead meat.

The protective hood shrivels in summer, leaving a fruit as large as a tennis ball with hard seeds inside that will be freed in the fall when the frost bursts the container. Large leaves then unfold and grow as large as platters.

PUSSY WILLOW

(Salix discolor)

The pussy willow is a harbinger of spring that appears very early, before the leaves unfold. The flowers, or fuzzy "pussies," develop on both male and female catkins, which grow on separate plants.

This species usually grows at marsh edges or other moist areas.

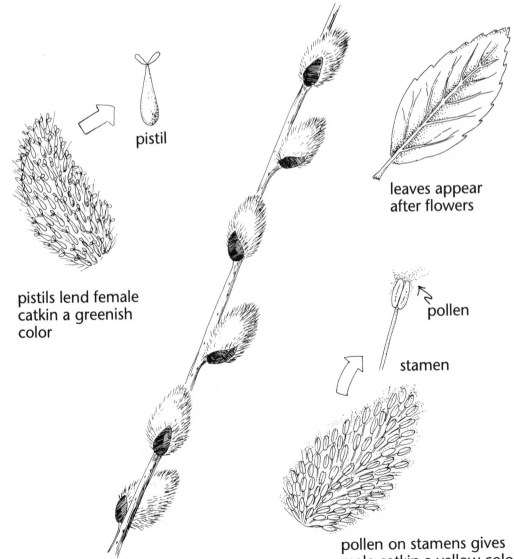

pistil

pistils lend female catkin a greenish color

leaves appear after flowers

pollen

stamen

pollen on stamens gives male catkin a yellow color

126

VIOLET

Marsh Blue Violet *(Viola cucullata)*

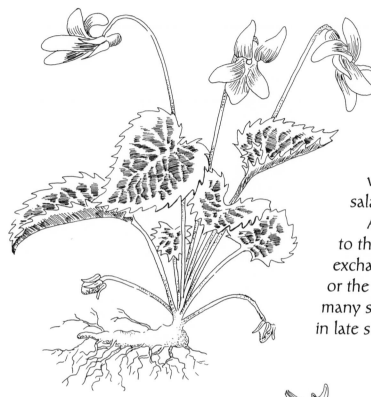

Violets bloom in early spring in shady, damp places. Flower colors range from violet to blue, green, yellow, and white.

The leaves and flowers are rich in vitamins A and C and can be eaten in salads.

An inconspicuous flower blooms low to the ground without opening. Pollen is exchanged inside without cross-fertilization or the help of insects. These flowers produce many seeds and shoot them out of the pod in late spring.

The colorful flowers attract insects to their sweet smell and bright color. Insects follow the nectar guides, tiny lines on the petals, to a small pocket, called the spur, in the center of the flower. When the insect lands on the spur, the long, thin, pollen-loaded stamens bend over and touch the insect. The pollen-dusted insect then visits another flower, inadvertently pollinating it.

nectar guides

127

BIBLIOGRAPHY

BOOKS

Allen, A., and Nick Dranas. 1964. *New York State Conservation Dept. Information Leaflet—Nests.* Albany, N.Y.: New York State Conservation Dept.

Borror, Donald J., and Richard E. White. 1970. *A Field Guide to Insects.* Boston: Houghton Mifflin Co.

Bull, John, and John Farrand Jr. 1977. *The Audubon Society Field Guide to North American Birds.* New York: Alfred A. Knopf Inc.

Cavendish, Marshall. 1979. *The Marshall Cavendish Illustrated Encyclopedia of Plants and Animals.* London, N.Y.: The Marshall Cavendish.

Chinery, Michael. 1977. *Enjoying Nature With Your Family.* New York: Crown Publishers Inc.

Conant, Roger. 1958. *A Field Guide to Reptiles and Amphibians of Eastern North America.* Boston: Houghton Mifflin Co.

DeJoode, Tom, and Anthony Stolk. 1982. *The Backyard Bestiary.* New York: Alfred A. Knopf Inc.

Doering, Harold. 1963. *A Bee is Born.* New York: Sterling Publishing Co., Inc.

Durrell, Gerald. 1986. *Amateur Naturalist.* New York: Alfred A. Knopf Inc.

Gibbon, Euell. 1962. *Stalking the Wild Asparagus.* New York: David McKay Co., Inc.

Gilhen, John. 1984. *Amphibians and Reptiles of Nova Scotia.* Haifax: Nova Scotia Museum.

Harrison, Hal H. 1975. *A Field Guide to Birds' Nests.* Boston: Houghton Mifflin Co.

Jason, Dan, Nancy Jason, and Dave Manning. 1972. *Some Useful Wild Plants.* Vancouver, B.C.: Talon Books.

Johnson, Sylvia A. 1980. *Mosses.* Minneapolis: Lerner Publications Co.

Karstan, Aleta. 1979. *Canadian Nature Notebook.* Toronto: McGraw-Hill Ryerson Ltd.

Lobsenz, Norman M. 1962. *The Insect World.* New York: Golden Press.

Marsh, Janet. 1979. *Nature Diary.* New York: Michael Joseph.

Mitchell, John Hanson. 1985. *A Field Guide to Your Own Backyard.* New York: W.W. Norton Co.

Mitchell, John, and the Massachusetts Audubon Society. 1980. *The Curious Naturalist.* New Jersey: Prentice-Hall, Inc.

Murie, Olaus J. A. 1974. *Field Guide to Animal Tracks.* Boston: Houghton Mifflin Co.

National Geographic Society. 1987. *Wild Animals of North America.* Washington, D.C.: National Geographic Society.

Niering, William A., and Nancy C. Olmstead. 1979. *The Audubon Society Field Guide to North American Wildflowers.* New York: Alfred A. Knopf Inc.

Palmer, E. Lawrence. 1949. *The Fieldbook of Natural History.* New York: McGraw-Hill Book Co.

Paysan, Klaus. 1971. *Creatures of Pond and Pool.* Minneapolis: Lerner Publishing Co.

Peterson, Roger Tory. 1974. *A Field Guide to Birds East of the Rockies.* Boston: Houghton Mifflin Co.

Petrides, George A. 1972. *A Field Guide to Trees and Shrubs.* Boston: Houghton Mifflin Co.

Readers Digest ABC's of Nature. 1984. Pleasantville, New York: Readers Digest Assoc.

Reynolds, John. 1974. *Bees and Wasps.* Chicago: Priory Press.

Rickett, Harold William. 1963. *The New Field Book of American Wildflowers.* New York: G. P. Putnam's Sons.

Robbins, Weier, Stocking. 1957. *Botany—An Introduction to Plant Science.* New York: John Wiley and Sons Inc.

Russell, Helen R. 1973. *Ten Minute Field Trips.* Chicago: J. G. Ferguson Publishing Co.

Selsam, Millicent E. 1984. *Where Do They Go? Insects in Winter.* New York: Four Winds Press.

Simon, Seymour. 1975. *Pets in a Jar.* New York: Viking Press.

Stein, Sara. 1986. *The Evolution Book.* New York: Workman Publishing.

Stewart, Anne Marie, and Leon Kronoff. 1975. *Eating from the Wild.* New York: Ballantine Books.

Stokes, Donald W. 1976. *A Guide to Nature in Winter.* Boston: Little, Brown & Co.

Sutton, Ann, and Myron Sutton. 1985. *The Audubon Society Field Guide—Eastern Forests.* New York: Alfred A. Knopf Inc.

Suziki, David, and Barbara Hehner. 1986. *Looking At Insects.* Toronto: Stoddart Publishing Co.

Tarrant, Graham, series editor. 1980. *Dragonflies—Oxford Scientific Films.* London: G. Whizzaid Publishing Ltd.

Zanetti, Andriano. 1978. *The World of Insects.* New York: Abbeville Press.

Zim, Herbert, and Clarence Cottam. 1956. *Insects: A Guide To Familiar American Insects.* New York: Golden Press.

MAGAZINES

Ranger Rick. Washington, D.C.: The National Wildlife Federation. Various issues from 1973 to 1987.

National Wildlife Magazine. Washington, D.C.: The National Wildlife Federation. Various issues from 1969 to 1987.

WHERE THE SPECIES DESCRIBED IN THIS BOOK CAN BE FOUND

Whenever a particular species is described, the distribution of the species, rather than of the general family, is given. For example, you will find the range of the little brown bat listed rather than that of bats in general.

Ants (family Formicidae): Worldwide in temperate regions.

Back Swimmer (genus *Notonecta*): One or another of the six varieties of this species can be found anywhere in the U.S. and southern Canada.

Bat, little brown bat *(Myotis lucifugus)*: Newfoundland and southern Quebec west to British Columbia coast and southern Alaska, south to Georgia, northern Texas, and northern California.

Beaver *(Castor canadensis)*: Most of Canada and the U.S. except Florida, much of Nevada, and southern California.

Bee, bumblebee (genus *Bombus*): Throughout the U.S. and southern Canada, especially abundant in central Mississippi Valley.

Bee, honeybee *(Apis mellifera)*: Worldwide.

Blackberry *(Rubus allegheniensis)*: Nova Scotia south to North Carolina and west to the Allegheny Mountains.

Blueberry, low bush *(Vaccinium angustifolium)*: Newfoundland to Saskatchewan, south to the uplands of Virginia and Ohio.

Bunchberry *(Cornus canadensis)*: From Minnesota, southern Canada, and Labrador south to South Dakota, Illinois, Ohio, West Virginia, and Maryland.

Butterfly, monarch *(Danaus plexippus)*: Most of southern Canada and the U.S.; winters in Mexico.

Butterfly, mourning cloak *(Nymphalis antiopa)*: Southeast Canada to the Midwest states (from the arctic circle to 30 degrees north latitude).

Caddis fly (order Trichoptera): Common throughout most of North America.

Cattail *(Typha latifolia)*: Temperate North America.

Chickadee, black capped *(Parus atricapillus)*: Breeds from Alaska to Newfoundland south to northern New Jersey and west to Missouri and northern California; winters south to Maryland and Texas.

Chipmunk, eastern *(Tamias striatus)*: Nova Scotia west to southern Manitoba and northeast North Dakota; south to Louisiana, northern Mississippi, Alabama, Georgia, western Carolinas, and eastern Virginia.

Clover, red *(Trifolium pratense)*: Labrador to British Columbia, south through the U.S.

Cottontail, eastern *(Sylvilagus floridanus)*: East of the Dakotas, Colorado, Texas, Mexico to the Atlantic Coast; north to New York, Massachusetts.

Coyote *(Canis latrans)*: From the western U.S. coast to East, except coastal areas of central and southeastern U.S.; north into Canada especially following northwest coast.

Cranberry, wild *(Vaccinium macrocarpon)*: Newfoundland and Nova Scotia south to North Carolina, west to Illinois, north to Minnesota.

Crow *(Corvus brachyrhynchos)*: Breeds from Newfoundland to British Columbia south to Florida's Gulf Coast and northern Mexico; winters north to southern Canada.

Cricket, field *(Gryllus assimilis)*: All North America to Alaska.

Daddy longlegs *(Liobum vittatum)*: East of the Rocky Mountains.

Damselfly, civil bluet *(Enallagma civile)*: Nova Scotia and Maryland west to Washington.

Dandelion *(Taraxacum officinale)*: Most of North America, rare in the southeastern U.S.

Deer, white-tailed *(Odocoileus virginianus)*: Southern half of Canada, most of the U.S. except most of California, Nevada, Utah, northern Arizona, southwestern Colorado, and northwest New Mexico.

Dragonfly, green darner *(Anax junius)*: Common throughout most of the U.S. and southern Canada and occurring in Alaska.

Earthworm *(Lumbricus terrestris)*: Temperate North America.

Elderberry *(Sambucus canadensis)*: Minnesota and Manitoba east to Nova Scotia, south to Florida, Louisiana, and Oklahoma.

Elm, American *(Ulmus americana)*: Newfoundland, Nova Scotia, eastern Quebec, and Saskatchewan south to northern Florida and Texas.

Fern, bracken *(Pteridium aquilinum)*: Newfoundland to Wyoming south to Florida and Arizona.

Firefly *(Photuris pennsylvanica)*: Atlantic coast to Texas, north to Manitoba.

Fox, red *(Vulpes vulpes)*: Most of Canada and the U.S. except much of the West Coast, northwestern Texas, coastal North Carolina, peninsular Florida, southwestern U.S., southern Alberta, and southeastern Saskatchewan to southwest Oklahoma.

Frog, bull *(Rana catesbeiana)*: Most of North America east of the Rockies; introduced west of the Rockies.

Frog, green *(Rana clamitans)*: Eastern North America from Nova Scotia to Florida.

Frog, gray tree *(Hyla versicolor)*: Maine to the Gulf States, west to Texas, Arkansas, and Minnesota.

Frog, leopard *(Rana pipiens)*: Southern Canada south to most of North America east of the Sierras.

Frog, pickerel *(Rana palustris)*: Hudson Bay south to Minnesota, Arkansas, Louisiana, and along the East Coast except for Florida and southeastern parts of Georgia and Alabama.

Frog, spring peeper *(Hyla crucifer)*: Nova Scotia and New Brunswick south to South Carolina; west to Louisiana, Arkansas, Kansas, and Manitoba.

Frog, wood *(Rana sylvatica)*: Nova Scotia south to South Carolina; west to Arkansas; north into Canada and Alaska except in the western U.S., southwestern Canada.

Fungus, white butt-rot *(Fomes applanatus)*: Found wherever its host trees (usually oak, poplar, beech, maple, birch, or elm) grow.

Galls: Wherever the host plants grow.

Garter snake *(Thamnophis sirtalis)*: Nova Scotia and eastern Canada west through Minnesota to British Columbia; south through most of the U.S. except the southwest desert.

Goldenrod, Canada *(Solidago canadensis)*: Newfoundland to Saskatchewan south to North Carolina, Tennessee, South Dakota, and New Mexico.

Gull, herring *(Larus argentatus)*: Breeds from Alaska and Greenland south to the Carolinas; winters south along the Atlantic coast.

Hornet, white-faced *(Vespa maculata)*: Vespidae family is abundant in eastern North America.

Horsetail *(Equisetum arvense)*: Newfoundland south to Alabama and west to Alaska and California.

Hummingbird, ruby-throated *(Archilochus colubris)*: Breeds from southeastern Canada to the Gulf Coast as far west as Texas; winters from Mexico and Panama north to the Gulf States.

Jack-in-the-pulpit *(Arisaema triphyllum)*: Nova Scotia and southern Quebec south through the Appalachians; south along the Atlantic Coast to Florida; and west to Louisiana and eastern Texas.

Jewelweed *(Impatiens capensis)*: Newfoundland west to Saskatchewan, south to Georgia, west to Oklahoma and Missouri.

Killdeer *(Charadrius vociferus)*: Breeds from Newfoundland and Mackenzie, British Columbia, south to West Indies, Mexico, and Peru; winters from New Jersey west to Ohio and south.

Ladybug, two-spotted *(Adalia bipunctata)*: Most of North America.

Lacewing, golden-eye *(Chrysopa occulata)*: Distributed throughout most of eastern North America.

Lichens: Throughout most of the world.

Mantis, praying *(Mantis religiosa)*: Most of the eastern U.S.

Maple, red *(Acer rubrum)*: Newfoundland, Ontario, and southeast Manitoba south to Florida and eastern Texas.

Maple, sugar (Acer saccharum): Newfoundland, Nova Scotia, and southwestern Quebec south to Virginia, northern Georgia, and Texas.

Milkweed (Asclepias syriaca): Parts of Nova Scotia and New Brunswick west to Saskatchewan; south to Georgia; west to Tennessee, Kansas, and Iowa.

Moles, star-nosed (Condylura cristata): Southern Labrador and Quebec west to southeastern Manitoba and northeastern Illinois, Ohio, and northeastern Michigan; south to Virginia, western North Carolina, and southeast Georgia.

Mosquito (Culex pipiens): Eastern North America and the Pacific Coast.

Moss, hair cap (Polytrichum commune): Most of the Northern Hemisphere.

Mouse, deer (Peromyscus maniculatus): Hudson Bay south to Pennsylvania; the Appalachians west to central Arkansas and central Texas; Mexico north to southern Yukon.

Mouse, white-footed (Peromyscus maniculatus): Maine and Great Lakes south except Florida and southern parts of South Carolina, Georgia, Alabama; west to eastern Arizona, eastern Colorado; north to Nebraska, Dakotas, and eastern Montana.

Newt, eastern (Notophthalmus viridescens): Nova Scotia south to Florida, west to southwestern Ontario and Texas.

Oak, red (Quercus rubra): Nova Scotia, southern Quebec, northern Michigan, northern Minnesota, and eastern Nebraska; south to Georgia and southeast Oklahoma.

Owl, great horned (Bubo virginianus): Arctic of North America south to Straits of Magellan, not including West Indies.

Partridge berry (Mitchella repens): Nova Scotia south to Florida, west to Texas, north to Minnesota.

Poison Ivy (Rhus radicans): Nova Scotia south to Florida, west to British Columbia, and south to Mexico.

Porcupine (Erethizon dorsatum): Most of Canada, northeastern U.S., West Coast of U.S.

Puffball, gemmed (Lycoperdon gemmatum): Throughout North America.

Pussy willow (Salix discolor): Newfoundland, Labrador, and British Columbia south to Delaware, Maryland, Missouri, and Idaho; south into the mountains of western North Carolina and eastern Tennessee.

Queen Anne's lace (Daucus carota): Coast to coast in North America.

Raccoon (Procyon lotor): Southern edges of Canada south into Mexico; East Coast to West Coast of the U.S., except portions of Rocky Mountains, central Nevada, and Utah.

Raspberry (Rubus strigosus): North Carolina and the Allegheny Mountains north into Canada and Alaska.

Robin (Turdus migratorius): Alaska east to Manitoba and Newfoundland; south to the Carolinas, Arkansas, and Guatemala; occasionally breeds along Gulf Coast; winters north to Newfoundland, southern Ontario and British Columbia.

Rose, Virginia (Rosa virginiana): Newfoundland, Nova Scotia, and southern Ontario south to Virginia, North Carolina, Alabama, and Tennessee; west to Missouri.

Serviceberry *(Amelanchier laevis):* Newfoundland to Ontario south through Nova Scotia, New England, Delaware, Georgia, Ohio, southern Indiana, and northern Illinois.

Shrew, northern short-tailed *(Blarina brevicauda):* Nova Scotia west to southern Saskatchewan; south to eastern Dakotas, eastern Texas, and Florida; north along the East Coast.

Skunk cabbage *(Symplocarpus foetidus):* Southern Canada, southern Nova Scotia, and northeastern U.S.; south to Georgia; west to Iowa.

Skunk, striped *(Mephitis mephitis):* Most of the U.S., southern half of Canada.

Slug, field gray *(Deroceras agreste):* Eastern U.S.

Sparrow, house *(Passer domesticus):* Now throughout temperate North America. Native to Eurasia and North Africa and introduced on all continents and many islands.

Spider, golden garden *(Argiope aurantia):* Throughout the U.S. and southern Canada.

Spittle bug *(Philaenus spumarius):* Abundant in eastern North America.

Squirrel, gray *(Sciurus carolinensis):* Nova Scotia and southern Ontario south to Florida, west to Texas, and north to Manitoba.

Strawberry, wild *(Fragaria virginiana):* Newfoundland south to Florida and west to Oklahoma and South Dakota.

Swallow, barn *(Hirundo rustica):* Alaska east to the Maritimes, south to Carolina, Arkansas, and Mexico; winters in South America. Also found in Eurasia.

Toad, American *(Bufo americanus):* Labrador, James Bay, Maritimes to southeastern Manitoba and Wisconsin; south to New England; from the Appalachian Mountains west to central Georgia, eastern Oklahoma, and Kansas.

Turtle, painted *(Chrysemys picta):* Nova Scotia west to British Columbia; south to Georgia and Louisiana; northwest to Oregon; isolated populations in the Southwest.

Violet, marsh blue *(Viola cucullata):* Newfoundland to British Columbia, south to Georgia and Tennessee.

Vole, meadow *(Microtus pennsylvanicus):* Across Canada except for the far north; south to the Carolinas, northeast Illinois, northeastern Kansas, Idaho, northeastern Washington.

Wasp, paper (genus *Polistes***):** Common throughout the U.S. and southern Canada.

Wasp, yellow mud-dauber *(Sceliphron coementarium):* Maritimes south to Florida, west to northern California, and north to Washington.

Water boatman (genus *Corixa***):** Found throughout the U.S. except the Southeast and the Gulf States.

Wintergreen *(Gaultheria procumbens):* Newfoundland south to Georgia and Alabama; north to Michigan, Wisconsin, Minnesota, and Manitoba.

Woodpecker, downy (*Picoides pubescens***):** Alaska east across Canada to Newfoundland, south to Gulf of Mexico.

Woolly caterpillar *(Isia isabella):* Most of the temperate U.S. and Canada.

INDEX

killdeer, 33
    nests of, 40

lacewing, golden-eye, 79
ladybug, two-spotted, 80
larch, 101
Larus argentatus, 31
lichens, 112-13
Liobum vittatum, 87
Lobaria pulmonaria, 112
Lumbricus terrestris, 58
Lycoperdon gemmatum, 122

mantid, European, 81
Mantis religiosa, 81
mantis, praying 81
    winter survival of, 25
maple
    gall on, 106
    red, 115
        leaf of, 114
    sugar, 116, 117
        leaf of, 114
maple syrup, 117
Mephitis mephitis, 17
Microtus pennsylvanicus, 12
midden, squirrel, definition of, 23
milkweed, common, 118
mink, tracks of, 20
Mitchella repens, 95
mole, star-nosed, 13
moose, evidence of, 23
mosquito, 82
moss, hair-cap, 119
    reindeer, 113
moth, Isabelle tiger, 86
    winter survival of, 25
mourning cloak. *See* butterfly, mourning
  cloak
mouse
    deer, 12
        tracks of, 19, 21
    evidence of, 22, 23
    jumping, winter hibernation of, 24
    remains of in owl pellets, 35
    white-footed, 12
muskrat, tracks of, 20
Myotis lucifugus, 3

newt, eastern, 52
niche, definition of, xiv
Notonecta species, 64
Notophthalmus viridescens, 52
Nymphales antiopa, 70

oak
    gall on, 106
    leaf of, 114
    red, 120
    white, 120
Odocoileus virginianus, 10-11
old man's beard, 113
opossum
    tracks of, 20
    winter dormancy of, 24
oriole, northern, nest of, 41
otter, tracks of, 20
owl
    great horned, 34
    pellets of, 35

pagoda lichens, 113
Parmelia physodes, 112
partridge berry, 95
Parus atricapillus, 29
Passer domesticus, 37
peeper, spring. *See* frog, spring peeper
Peromyscus leucopus, 12
    maniculatus, 12
pheasant, tracks of, 21
Philaenus spumarius, 83
Photuris pennsylvanica, 77
Picoides pubescens, 39
pine, 101
pixie cup lichens, 113
plants, edible, 95-97, 99, 102, 104, 108,
  110, 122, 124, 127
Polistes species, 85
Polytrichum commune, 119
poplar, gall on, 107
porcupine, 14
    tracks of, 20
praying mantis. *See* mantis, praying
porcupine, evidence of, 23
Procyon lotor, 15
Pteridium aquilinum, 104
puffball, gemmed, 122

141

ABOUT THE AUTHOR

Peggy Kochanoff has spent countless hours exploring and sketching the fields and woods of eastern Canada and the northeastern United States. Her fine drawings of plants and animals grace the pages of a botanical encyclopedia produced by Cornell University, English and Canadian horticultural publications, and brochures on Canada's national parks and forests. A graduate of Cornell University with a degree in vertebrate zoology, Kochanoff lives in Falmouth, Nova Scotia, where she and her husband operate a landscaping and nursery business.

144